Visions and Revelations
in the Spiritual Life

Fr. Gabriel of St. Mary Magdalen, O.C.D.

Visions and Revelations

SPIRITUAL DIRECTION
❧ SERIES ❧

SOPHIA INSTITUTE PRESS

Manchester, New Hampshire

Nihil obstat: R. D. Benedictus Adams, O.S.B., *Censor Deputatus*
Imprimatur: R. R. D. Herbertus Byrne, O.S.B., Abbas Praes.
June 2, 1949
Nihil obstat: Jacobus Bastible, *Censor Deputatus*
Imprimatur: ✠ Daniel, Episcopus Corcagiensis
June 22, 1950

Sophia Institute Press
Box 5284, Manchester, NH 03108
1-800-888-9344
www.SophiaInstitute.com

Sophia Institute Press is a registered trademark of Sophia Institute.

paperback ISBN 978-1-64413-718-5

ebook ISBN 978-1-64413-718-5

Library of Congress Control Number: 2022934366

First printing

Contents

Foreword

*My heart hath said to thee: "My face hath sought
thee: thy face, O Lord, will I still seek."*

—Psalm 26:8

Since the Resurrection of Jesus, people have desired to seek His
face, both in prayer and in their current age of history. Until
His coming at the end of time, Jesus comes to us in His Church
through the public revelation she teaches and proclaims. Public
revelation consists of the contents of Scripture and Tradition,
which it is necessary to believe for our salvation. These are more
than intellectual truths: they are divine mysteries that forge a sturdy
bridge across time and convey the graces of salvation and union
with God. Each believer is called to traverse that bridge of faith
in mind and heart, both in prayer and in his way of life, through
whose ordinary mysteries he is led to the person of Jesus Christ.
The Second Vatican Council speaks of public revelation in the
following way: "Jesus perfected revelation by fulfilling it through
his whole work of making Himself present and manifesting Himself: through His words and deeds, His signs and wonders, but
especially through His death and glorious resurrection from the

dead and final sending of the Spirit of truth."[1] The *Catechism of the Catholic Church* also speaks of the nature of public revelation, ending with the death of the last apostle:

> "The Christian economy, therefore, since it is the new and definitive Covenant, will never pass away; and no new public revelation is to be expected before the glorious manifestation of our Lord Jesus Christ."[2] Yet even if Revelation is already complete, it has not been made completely explicit; it remains for Christian faith gradually to grasp its full significance over the course of the centuries. (no. 66)

In living the life of faith throughout the Church's history, various members of the baptized faithful have reported experiencing the phenomenon of private revelations. Pope Benedict XVI tells us this:

> Private revelation is an aid to this faith, and it demonstrates credibility precisely because it refers back to the one public revelation. Ecclesiastical approval of a private revelation essentially means that its message contains nothing contrary to faith and morals; it is licit to make it public and the faithful are authorized to give to it their prudent adhesion.[3]

Well-known private revelations have been given to St. Juan Diego on Tepeyac Hill in Mexico; to St. Margaret Mary Alacoque in Paray Le Monial, France; to St. Bernadette Soubirous in Lourdes, France; to three shepherd children in Fatima, Portugal; and to St.

---

[1] Second Vatican Council, Dogmatic Constitution on Divine Revelation *Dei Verbum* (November 18, 1965), no. 4.

[2] *DV* 4; cf. 1 Tim. 6:14; Titus 2:13.

[3] Pope Benedict XVI, Post-Synodal Apostolic Exhortation *Verbum Domini* (September 30, 2010), no. 14.

Faustina Kowalska in Poland. Lesser-known private revelations have
been given by God to various members of the faithful in visions,
in locutions, in prayer, and in other ways. Authentic private revelations do not add or subtract from public revelation and should
not take our eyes away from what Jesus taught in the Gospels or
from what His Catholic Church teaches through her Magisterium.
Pope Benedict XVI notes further:

> A private revelation can introduce new emphases, give rise
> to new forms of piety, or deepen older ones. It can have a
> certain prophetic character (cf. 1 Th 5:19-21) and can be a
> valuable aid for better understanding and living the Gospel
> at a certain time; consequently it should not be treated
> lightly. It is a help which is proffered, but its use is not
> obligatory. In any event, it must be a matter of nourishing
> faith, hope and love, which are for everyone the permanent
> path of salvation.[4]

The rise of fascination in private revelations has coincided
with the fascination with the receiving of visions and revelations
in personal prayer. These phenomena are often the same as private
revelations but can occur on a lesser scale in the ordinary mysticism proper to the life of prayer that is open to all the baptized.
Such phenomena have been the object of scientific, psychological,
and theological inquiry throughout the history of the Church.
Nearly a century ago, Fr. Gabriel of Saint Mary Magdalen, the
renowned Discalced Carmelite priest, spiritual director, theologian,
and author, spoke of the danger of this unchecked curiosity and
fascination with visions, revelations, and locutions in the interior
life that pervades even our own age. If such a curiosity and focus

[4] *Verbum Domini*, no. 14.

is not restrained by the pastors of the Church and others who are charged with the care of souls, these dispositions can lead to both pseudo-mysticism and Gnosticism. Such dangerous and heretical tendencies can not only distort the message of the gospel but can also undermine the unity of the Church and the salvation of souls.[5] The problem of the unbridled fascination with and desire for visions and revelations in prayer then poses two questions of great pastoral concern for the care of souls: *How are priests and spiritual directors called to accompany and help people discern visions and revelations that they may receive in prayer? What is the place of such messages in the path of a particular person's journey with God in faith and the interior life?*

Two great Doctors of the Church from the Carmelite Tradition who wisely and prudently examine the hunger in prayer to seek the face of the Lord and hear His voice in the interior life are St. John of the Cross and St. Teresa of Ávila. *Visions and Revelations* by Fr. Gabriel of Saint Mary Magdalen explores their understanding of the various kinds of visions and locutions one can receive in the life of prayer. In this book—given originally as a series of lectures at the Teresianum in Rome from 1938 to 1939—Fr. Gabriel shows the unity of discernment in Teresa's mystical experiences in her prayer life and John's practical theological advice regarding visions and revelations received in prayer. In exploring the great spiritual works of these two Doctors of the Church, Fr. Gabriel

---

[5] See Pope Francis, Apostolic Exhortation *Gaudete et Exultate* (April 9, 2018), nos. 36–62; Congregation for the Doctrine of the Faith, *Norms regarding the Manner of Proceeding in the Discernment of Presumed Apparitions and Revelations* (February 25, 1978), and Congregation for the Doctrine of Faith, Letter *Placuit Deo*: To the Bishops of the Catholic Church on Certain Aspects of Christian Salvation (February 22, 2018).

offers timeless wisdom on how to approach visions and revelations in guiding souls who seek to live the interior lives faithfully. Such advice encourages a position of guarded openness in souls who encounter visions and revelations as well as in spiritual directors who guide those who experience these things in prayer. Fr. Gabriel explains how both St. John of the Cross and St. Teresa of Ávila show in their writings that visions and revelations are secondary elements in the life of faith lived through prayer. They are valuable only insofar as they lead us to divine union with God through prayer and faith. Insofar as we embrace visions and revelations as ends in themselves for our own gratification and pride, we risk being dangerously distracted or turned away from the Lord by a mercenary love that cuts us off from His divine embrace.

Fr. Gabriel, in this work, shows the unity of the wisdom that Teresa and John give us through their pastoral approach to mysticism in prayer rooted in wisdom, prudence, and thinking with the Church. He also shows how St. John's *no admitir* (do not receive them) approach is not a negative repression of what one experiences in prayer. It refocuses the heart on the ultimate truth and mystery that the extraordinary gifts that the Lord can bestow on a person in prayer are meant to foster union with Him through faith, hope, and love. This principle also shows us that when God gives these gifts to a soul, they often can convey a deeper and higher meaning that we can easily forsake or overlook through an overly literal and self-centered view of them. John's *no admitir* teaching, then, leads to the development of an authentic reverence toward the stirrings of grace that foster a union of love between God and the soul.

I originally read this book during my final year at St. Joseph's Seminary in Yonkers, New York, while writing my master's thesis, titled " 'Testing the Spirits': On the Principles of Discerning Private Revelations according to Scripture, the Teachings of the

Magisterium, and the Teaching of the Carmelite School of Spirituality." I have found this book an invaluable resource to my own study of the writings of St. John of the Cross and St. Teresa of Ávila as well as to the souls to whom I have the privilege to minister both in Confession and in spiritual direction.

To this new edition of *Visions and Revelations* by Fr. Gabriel of St. Mary Magdalen, O.C.D., we have added two appendices: "Recent Magisterial Teaching on the Discernment of Visions and Revelations" and "Other Pastoral Considerations in the Discernment of Visions and Revelations." This book is meant to equip priests, spiritual directors, teachers of theology, retreat masters, and those involved with exorcism and deliverance ministry with the tools to discern and to accompany souls on the path to union with Christ through prayer and to guard against deceptions.

May the work of St. John of the Cross, St. Teresa of Ávila, and Fr. Gabriel of St. Mary Magdalen continue to guide souls along the way to union with God through living the interior life. May it help them attune their hearts so they may truly see the face of the Lord and hear His voice while guarding against all the distractions and deceptions that seek to lure them away from His eternal embrace.

–Fr. Matthew MacDonald, S.T.B., M.Div., M.A. Theol.

Preface

This book is intended as a further contribution to the solution of the problems presented by the direction of souls leading a specially interior life.

With this study—first offered to the public in the form of conferences in the lecture hall of Santa Teresa, in Rome, during the years 1938 and 1939—we face a matter of the delicacy and difficulty of which we are not unaware. The attitude of the interior soul and of its director toward those strange, and often attractive, phenomena known as visions and revelations has, during the course of centuries, been the object of scientific inquiry on the part of many mystical theologians. Although the attitude of these mental scientists with respect to such extraordinary graces has become increasingly severe, nevertheless, we cannot say that, among spiritual persons, an attitude of prudence in regard to these matters is as yet general. Even in our own day, there is too much credulity in this department, and it is a credulity that leads to deplorable consequences, which are inimical to the real progress of the spiritual life.

We think it useful, therefore, to give a wider diffusion to the teaching of a saint who has treated of this subject organically. St. John of the Cross, the great Doctor of union with God, has shown, with incomparable clarity, that the way to such intimate divine union is faith, whereas visions and revelations are shown to be secondary elements, full of danger. Souls must be warned off a way exposed to delusions. Esteem and love of the way of faith does not lead to credulity; it even excludes the latter more decisively.

We have thought well, also, to make use in our studies of the most recent conclusions of psychological science. If not all of these can be considered as finally fixed positions, they make it clear that the development of modern sciences tends ever increasingly to justify the attitude assumed by the shrewd and enlightened intuition of the Mystical Doctor.

If these lectures serve the better to convince spiritual persons that they should not lose valuable time, owing to a too great esteem for and preoccupation with such favors, we shall consider that ours has been profitably spent for their welfare and for the glory of God.

—Fr. Gabriel of St. Mary Magdalen,
Discalced Carmelite
Rome, July 16, 1940

Introduction

In our times, mysticism is the order of the day. We hear it discussed almost everywhere. Its concept, however, seems to have acquired a certain elasticity, since, although at first limited to the supernatural order, it is now extended to the natural. Indeed, certain political movements talk about their "mysticism," and enough has been written upon the mystical aspect of communism. But the incon-venience of elastic concepts is that they are not sufficiently precise; and sometimes their frequent use gives rise to a great confusion of ideas that may lead to lamentable consequences in practice. Especially when the spiritual life is in question, to misunderstand certain fundamental concepts may be to cause souls to go astray disastrously. For this reason, it is necessary to state precisely the meaning of the usual Catholic phraseology and not to extend unduly the meaning of expressions consecrated by Christian tradi-tion. A recent encyclical has well brought out the wisdom of this rule, which is dictated by simple good sense.[6]

But even while reserving to the concept of "mysticism" its supernatural meaning, it cannot be said that this is so determined for everybody as always to indicate the same reality. It is true,

---

[6] *Acta Apostolicae Sedis* (1937): 156.

and we are sincerely glad thereof, that in the abundant Catholic spiritual reading of our day, the word "mysticism" normally means the infused contemplation of God that, as it develops, leads the soul to the heights of the Transforming Union with Him, but it is impossible to believe that this acceptation of the word has, as yet, become general in all religious circles. Only too often still, by a "mystic" is understood a man who converses familiarly with the supernatural world and receives open communications therefrom; that is to say, a man favored with visions and revelations. For many people of mediocre religious culture, a mystic is an extraordinary individual who lives a very different sort of life from that of the ordinary Christian. He sees Heaven opened and is continually receiving visits from its inhabitants, who even direct him in his conduct. He is a sort of intermediary, a mediator between God and men, who transmits to the latter orders or communications from God. He is, as it were, an "oracle" to whom men must hearken with reverence and docility.

At times, we have seen some religious community disturbed by the predictions of some too-much-admired visionary, whose predictions in the event have not been fulfilled; and this sort of thing has occasionally contributed to cast a certain discredit upon mysticism, as though it were something trivial and good only for people of weak intellect. Such was certainly the opinion of a mother who, when recommending her daughter to the prioress of a certain Carmel the girl wished to enter, said: "Mother, my Jane has a head on her shoulders. You can be quite easy; she will never be a mystic!" Such deplorable misunderstandings should be avoided. "Mystic" is not synonymous with "visionary."

Notwithstanding, we have no wish to assert that visions and revelations, if authentic, are not mystical graces. They have their place in the mystical life and, as we shall see later, even an estimable place; but we wish to demonstrate clearly, making use of Teresian teaching, that this place is entirely *secondary and accidental.* Hence, such graces cannot be considered as the characteristic of the mystical life. We must get rid, once and for all, of this wholly mistaken idea that, in practice, gives rise to serious errors.

In recent years, it has been emphatically asserted by many theologians—and we have shown elsewhere that such is also the opinion of the Teresian school[7]—that interior souls may cherish a contemplative ideal and order their lives with a view to attaining to mystical union with God. Those, however, who confuse the mystical life with visions and revelations may believe that it is right to aspire to these immediate communications with God and the saints, which seem to have a particular attraction for certain people, and this would be to expose themselves to many delusions. Indeed, in order to fall into these dangers, it is not even necessary to confuse the mystical life with visions; it suffices to ignore the fact that, with respect to these extraordinary graces, the soul must take up a very different attitude from that which it adopts toward contemplation. I think we may assert that, on this point, practically speaking there is still great ignorance.

In many cases, there is an exaggerated esteem for these heavenly favors, as they are considered to be, and this esteem is forthwith extended from the graces themselves to the persons who believe themselves so favored. Undoubtedly they are saints! All the opinions of these souls, so enlightened by God, must be taken seriously! When a director becomes thus enthusiastic over his Philothea, the roles are interchanged, and it is the visionary who becomes the director, while the priest submits himself as the docile disciple of

---

[7] See Fr. Gabriel of St. Mary Magdalen, O.C.D., *St. John of the Cross: Doctor of Divine Love and Contemplation* (Cork: Mercier Press, 1946).

his spiritual child. Many an imprudence usually follows in consequence. Some go so far as to inquire of the Lord, by means of the
visionary, concerning the conduct of their lives and their priestly
activity. Woe be to whoever contradicts or hinders directions that
have come straight from Heaven!

In the whole of this field, there is still too much credulity, alike
on the part of directors as on that of the directed. A craving for the
marvelous seems innate in many people, and this inclines them
to pronounce supernatural, without any critical sense, everything
that in the spiritual order verges upon the extraordinary. We must
not forget that man carries about with him all the idiosyncrasies
of his own nature, even into his spiritual life, and the religious
coloring wherewith he paints certain morbid phenomena does
not alter their worthlessness.

It must be said that even in his spiritual life, man cannot lay
aside his good common sense and prudence. Since it is true that
religious values are supreme, it even behooves us to walk there with
more circumspection than elsewhere. The more valuable a form
of life may be, the more care must be taken to avoid anything that
might injure its normal development. Since the office of spiritual
theology is to guide souls through their spiritual lives in the best
way, to lead them to perfection as soon as may be, it must point
out to them the obstacles they may meet on the road and how
best to avoid stumbling over these. Therefore, we cannot exempt
ourselves from the obligation of treating also the delicate matter
of visions and revelations.

We have willingly undertaken to expound these problems,
since, in the teachings of St. John of the Cross and his school, we
find a complete and lucid solution of all the questions involved.

St. Teresa of Jesus, with her wide experience of supernatural
favors and her very precise psychological descriptions, will furnish

us with ample material, and that of the first quality, in order that we may form a clear idea of the phenomena that we have to examine, notwithstanding the fact that we have never had personal experience of such. And, after all, for the direction of souls endowed with such graces, there could be no safer teaching than that of the saint whose authority has been officially recognized by Holy Church. Moreover, this teaching of St. John has not only been adopted by the numerous company of theologians who form the well-known Teresian mystical school but has spread beyond the latter. In fact, at the present day, it even tends to become increasingly common among Catholic mystical writers. Nevertheless, it is not always expounded with all due clarity, and hence, we do not think it superfluous to expound it afresh so as to contribute to its more general diffusion.

In the first chapter of this book, we shall show how the place to be assigned to the phenomena in question in the spiritual life is really accidental and secondary.

In the second, after examining the various problems arising out of the visions, we shall determine the nature of the question that more directly concerns spiritual theology.

In the third, St. John of the Cross will teach us what should be the soul's attitude toward these favors.

In the fourth, we shall explain how the director should behave in regard to souls favored with such graces.

Visions and Revelations in the Development of the Spiritual Life

Hagiography is much cultivated by Catholic writers and, since it is a human undertaking, besides its merits it has also its weak points. One of the defects from which biographers of saints have most frequently suffered is that of having overemphasized those details in the lives of their subjects that presented an appearance of the marvelous. It is the everlasting admiration of man for that which surpasses his capacities, joined, in the cases of certain writers, to a kind of need—I would say a mania—for showing in the lives of saints the *extraordinary* intervention of God. Yet they ought to realize how, by attributing to extraordinary intervention all that is finest in their Christian heroes, they are, in fact, contributing to undervalue the care wherewith the ordinary general providence of God urges souls on to the heights of sanctity.

It is this defect that has frequently led writers of lives of the saints to give an exaggerated importance to their visions and revelations. Many authors think that their subjects will prove more attractive to the minds of the readers if they can state that, from their infancy, those subjects had continual relations with their angel guardians or, better still, with the Child Jesus! If, subsequently, it can be added that, throughout their lives, they were constantly being directed by messages from Heaven, their holiness will be perfect! Yet, creatures such as these, who come into the world surrounded by an atmosphere of special privilege, must be objects of admiration rather than of imitation, unless we also ought to beseech God to endow us with similar privileges. And indeed, if these be the characteristics of sanctity, is it not right that such as would be saints should desire them? And should we meet with some soul enjoying such favors, must we not believe that we are in the presence of a saint, at least "in the making"?

In order to reply adequately to such and other similar questions, in this first chapter we shall examine, in the light of Teresian doctrine, what place precisely belongs to the phenomena known as "visions" and "revelations" in the supernatural life.

⌒

The spiritual teaching of the Teresian Carmel urges souls on along the road of the highest sanctity, toward the most intimate union that can be reached in this world between the soul and God. Two great saints, universally recognized as "princes" of mystical theology, have codified in their works the principles along which they trained the spiritual family that God entrusted to them; and they have described the graces with which God commonly endows the soul that generously sets itself to seek Him. Teresa the Great and John of the Cross have traced out the itinerary of the soul in its spiritual ascension up in the loftiest peaks of sanctity. What is the place assigned in this itinerary to visions and revelations?

St. Teresa's Teaching

Let us first question St. Teresa, who treats at length of these particular graces in her different works. We shall step straight into

The Interior Castle, the saint's masterpiece, in which her teaching is to be found in its most synthetic form.

When she wrote it, Teresa was sixty-two years of age — mature in years and experience. Five years previously, she had reached the summit of the mystical life, the Spiritual Marriage. During fifteen years, she had written much, both in order to guide her own nuns, to whom God had granted great graces in prayer, and in order to give an account of her soul to her directors. A keen observer, endowed with no common skill in introspection and with remarkable clearness in expressing herself, Teresa possessed all the requisite qualities to enable her to describe perfectly the development of the supernatural life, as she knew it from her personal experience and observed it in her daughters, whose confidences she received. In fact, her descriptions are admittedly so rich and precise that Teresa has truly renewed one of the basic studies of mystical science — that is, the clear determining of the phenomena experienced by mystical souls. When we want to know what we should understand by visions and revelations, we find the saint's works are a very valuable source of information. For the moment, however, we are only inquiring of her whether these favors are strictly bound up with the development of the contemplative spiritual life.

As a help in finding the answer, we may run briefly through the book.

The Interior Castle consists of seven sets of apartments, or mansions.[8] In the last, the soul has reached the term of the mystical life — that is to say, perfect and continual union with God. All the other mansions lead gradually to this termination. In the first three, the soul, still a novice in the supernatural life, practices

---

[8] In Spain, the book is always known as the *Mansions*. — Trans.

mental prayer. The form of its relations with God has a *mode* that is quite natural. It reflects upon revealed truths that make known to us God's loving-kindness and the requirements that His service involves; then the will resolves to correspond to God's invitation, to render Him love for love, and to show that love by serving Him generously. Since it does not mean to do things by halves but desires to reach the high goal of sanctity as quickly as possible, the soul sets out on its spiritual journey with vigorous energy. To that it must adhere if it would travel rapidly and climb high. However, its mental prayer is still *meditation*.

With the Fourth Mansion begins that intensifying of the spiritual life that is commonly called the *Illuminative Way*, and the saint speaks to us here of *contemplation*. The relations of the soul with God simplify. Little by little, there comes upon it a gentle recollection, and meditation disappears. The soul must now simply remain in God's company and, moreover, God comes to its assistance. First, He seizes upon its will, fixing it, drawing it into His love, and flooding it with a peace that is sometimes extended to all the interior powers and even to the whole person. Then gradually the understanding and the memory are increasingly enveloped by the divine infusion. Absorbed in the practice of contemplation, in a kind of "sleep of the powers," the soul experiences moments of real beatitude. Here is the whole development of prayer in the Illuminative Way.[9] We are standing on the threshold of the Unitive Way, and Teresa has not spoken even a word with reference to visions and revelations.

[9] For a more detailed description of these graces, see Fr. Gabriel of St. Mary Magdalen, O.C.D., *St. Teresa, Mistress of the Spiritual Life*, trans. a Benedictine of Stanbrook Abbey (Cork: Mercier Press, 1949).

With the Fifth Mansion begins the Unitive Way. The soul now receives the prayer of union. This is an experience of an action of God so deep that "when the soul returns to itself, it cannot doubt that God has been in it and it in God."[10] The prayer of union, however, is a transitory grace that should increase both in intensity and in duration. For this reason, St. Teresa compares it to the first of the three phases that mark the conclusion of a marriage: the first addresses, the betrothal, and the actual nuptial union. Consequently, further progress has yet to be made; two more series of mansions have yet to be gone through: that of the betrothal and that of the Spiritual Marriage. The saint has studied both of these in all their particular details. We must stay a while here with her, for we shall here find what we are seeking.

The description of the Sixth Mansion takes up more than a third of *The Interior Castle*. In order to explain such lengthy treatment, it is well to note that St. Teresa spent fifteen years of her life in this mansion, whereas, reckoning from the time of her final conversion, she does not seem to have spent more than two years in the Fourth and Fifth mansions. The exposition of these in the *Castle* is decidedly brief. On the other hand, the description of the Sixth Mansion promises to be specially interesting.

The grace that seems to be there shown as the principal and central one is that of *rapture*, which is an intensified form of the prayer of union, characteristic of the preceding mansion. In fact, rapture is also a kind of union in which the soul is deeply plunged in God, in such a manner as to remain fully certain that it was with Him; but this time, the immersion in God becomes so intense that the soul is deprived of the use of its senses. It is precisely for this reason that such experience is called "rapture."

---

[10] *The Interior Castle* [hereafter, *Castle*], Fifth Mansion, chap.1.

Visions and Revelations

This principal favor is accompanied by many others. In the opening chapters of her study, St. Teresa explains different ways whereby the soul is prepared for the grace of rapture. These are, above all, the trials wherewith God tests the soul's fidelity, since He desires to make it His betrothed. Sufferings within and without reduce the soul to a condition of distress and darkness from which there seems no way out. Together with the trials there come God's invitations. Vehement, loving impulses wound the soul, causing it to complain because of the earnest longing for union that they arouse within it, but all these divine invitations do not take the same form. "There is another manner in which God wills to arouse souls," says the saint. "It may seem that in some ways there is question of a greater grace than the former, but as we may be liable to greater dangers, I wish to speak of it a little more at length. *It is a matter of certain words which God speaks to the soul.* Some seem to come from without, others from the most secret depths of the soul; others from its highest point and others from outside, in the way we hear them with our bodily ears, and seem as though they were uttered by a human voice."[11]

This time, we have arrived! Here she is speaking of what are commonly known as revelations, or supernatural locutions, and to these, Teresa assigns the function of preparing the soul for a closer union with God. But this is not all, for we shall meet also with visions.

In fact, while the saint is explaining the nature of rapture, lo! there appear the imaginary and intellectual visions that sometimes accompany that state.[12] "When the soul is in this state of suspension, and the Lord sees fit to reveal to it certain mysteries, such as heavenly secrets and imaginary visions, it is able subsequently

[11] *Castle*, Sixth Mansion, chap. 3.
[12] *Castle*, Sixth Mansion, chap. 3.

to describe them.... But when they are intellectual visions they cannot be so described."[13]

Hence, in rapture we meet with two kinds of visions: imaginary and intellectual. It is true that these intellectual visions that the soul is "unable to describe" may be simple manifestations of the divine attributes; manifestations that belong rather to the order of very high infused contemplation than to that of visions, properly so called,[14] but a little further on, the saint tells us of an intellectual vision of the humanity of Our Lord.

> In order, Sisters, that you may know more clearly ... that the further a soul progresses, the closer becomes its companionship with this good Jesus, it will be well for us to consider how, when His Majesty so wills, we cannot do otherwise than stay with Him all the time. This happens by means of such wonderful appearances and visions. Should the Lord grant you any of the favors which I shall describe (I mean, if He grants me ability to describe any of them) you need not be dismayed.[15]

Here we have St. Teresa bidding us not to be frightened if, someday, we also receive some vision! She is speaking, however, to souls that have reached ecstatic prayer of union, which normally supposes that they are walking apace by the Unitive Way and are, in consequence, really perfect. We shall have occasion to explain, further on, how sanctity and the high mystical prayer that often accompanies it are an excellent guarantee of the authenticity of

---

[13] *Castle*, Sixth Manion, chap. 4
[14] St. John of the Cross, *Ascent of Mount Carmel* [hereafter, *Ascent*], bk. 2, chap. 26.
[15] *Castle*, Sixth Mansion, chap. 8.

the visions. This explains how the saint can tranquilize the soul that has attained to this height.

And yet, there remains another stage at which the soul may arrive in this life. There is still the Seventh Mansion, wherein the Spiritual Marriage takes place. Here also, the saint mentions intellectual visions. When led into the Seventh Mansion, the soul sees itself continually in the company of the Most Holy Trinity. "The Three Persons are seen individually, and by a wonderful kind of knowledge which is given to it, the soul knows most certainly and truly that all Three Persons are one Substance, and one Power, one Knowledge and one God."[16] In this wondrous company, the Spiritual Marriage is celebrated. "The Lord appears in the center of the soul, not through an imaginary but through an intellectual vision.... This is so great a secret and so sublime a favour ... that I do not know with what to compare it.... It is impossible to say more than that, as far as we can understand, the soul—I mean the spirit of the soul— is made one with God."[17] Wholly renewed, to the very depths of its being, the soul cries out: *Mihi vivere Christus est!* It breaks out into tenderly loving expressions: "Oh, life of my life! Oh, sustenance that sustains me!"[18] In these sublime pages, the most expressive figures of speech, all significant of abundance and riches, pour forth tumultuously from Teresa's pen, incapable of conveying an adequate idea of the life that she feels welling up from the center of her soul. It is Heaven on Earth. The soul rejoices in the presence of the Trinity and delights itself with its Bridegroom, Christ Jesus.

So, does it not seem that the highest mystical life must end in visions?

[16] *Castle,* Seventh Mansion, chap. 1.
[17] *Castle,* Seventh Mansion, chap. 1.
[18] *Castle,* Seventh Mansion, chap. 1.

The Teaching of St. John of the Cross

For the spiritual director, it is a serious problem! As a prudent man, knowing that visions expose the visionary to deceptions, he has advised a little moderation to his spiritual child who, full of delight, has come to relate to him how she has seen the Child Jesus! But he does not find her very docile. With an obstinacy often characteristic of visionaries, she retorts: "But, Father, why are you so opposed to me? St. Teresa also had visions that made a saint of her! Why cannot I walk by the same road? It is the way of holiness!" What ought the director to reply?

In any case, he might answer: "My child, if you want to become a saint, begin first of all by being a little more humble, and learn to obey." But he may also combat the misconception under which his penitent is lying, and for that he has excellent reasons.

Is it really true that the way of visions and revelations is the way of holiness? Let us ask St. John of the Cross, Mystical Doctor not only of Carmel but of the universal Church. Doubtless a little light will come to us from that quarter.

St. John, also, has mapped out in his works the mystical itinerary of the soul that is climbing up to the highest peaks of the Transforming Union and the Spiritual Marriage.

The Holy Doctor fits his exposition into the traditional three-fold division of the spiritual journey into the Purgative, Illuminative, and Unitive Ways. Each of these ways has its characteristic exercises. In the first, the soul applies itself directly to the mortification of the senses and passions and sustains its voluntary effort with frequent meditations that lead on to generous resolutions. In order to lead it into the Illuminative way, in which its mental prayer takes on the form of a simple and obscure contemplation, God causes the soul to go through a trying period of aridity, during which it learns in practice to seek God with the spirit rather than with the senses; whereas, at the beginning of its conversion, it was often drawn by sensible affection, it now becomes truly "spiritual." It is nourished especially by an intensive practice of the theological virtues, which, according to St. John, are *the most direct and most intimate means* of attaining to union with God.

So far, the teaching of the Mystical Doctor is perfectly in accord with that of St. Teresa, but at this point, he deduces from the premises a very important conclusion, which must be held as fundamental through all his teaching: if the way that leads directly to God is that of the theological virtues, it is not right to support our spiritual life on visions and revelations; we must detach ourselves from them and, as far as possible, reject them. Listen to the urgent words of the Mystical Doctor: "The soul that is pure, cautious, simple and humble, must resist revelations and other visions with as much effort and care as though they were very perilous temptations; for there is no need to desire them. On the contrary, there is need not to desire them, if we are to reach the union of love."[19]

On hearing this pronouncement, our good visionary will, perhaps, feel a little less secure, yet if he or she be at all shrewd, an objection may be raised. We grant, certainly, that the soul ought not to attach any importance to visions until it has attained to union with God but, from St. Teresa's descriptions, it seems evident that in the higher mansions, those of the Spiritual Betrothal and Marriage, the soul may be favored with abundant supernatural communications. When plunged in ecstasy, it receives intellectual and imaginary visions; in the Seventh Mansion, it enjoys visions of the Blessed Trinity and of Our Lord Jesus Christ. Is the Mystical Doctor perhaps going to contradict what is taught by the great

---

[19] *Ascent*, bk. 2, chap. 27.

saint who was also his spiritual mother? We proceed to examine what he teaches with respect to these higher mystical states.

St. John of the Cross has treated of the Spiritual Betrothal and Marriage with a thoroughness certainly not inferior to that of St. Teresa. His study of the Marriage, in particular, is much more extensive than hers. It is enough to recall that the whole book of the *Living Flame of Love* — apart from one important digression — is devoted to expounding those graces that belong to the state of the Spiritual Marriage. For St. John, as for St. Teresa, in this state the soul lives in a very intimate relation with God. More profoundly than does she, he explains how the soul is "one single spirit with the Lord." And yet there is never any question either of a vision of the Trinity or of one of Our Lord. When St. John describes the high contemplative experiences of a soul transformed in God, he mentions also manifestations of the divine attributes made to the soul[20] and even of a profound understanding of the relations of God with the world[21] and of the more sublime mysteries of the Incarnation and Redemption.[22] But rather than visions properly so called, all these graces seem to be profound experiences of the soul, which, in some way, shares in the redemptive mystery of Christ, and as it were, feels the overshadowing of the divine perfections in the wealth of the spiritual life that is communicated to it. Indeed, when speaking of them, St. John never uses the word "visions." It is true that he does employ the word "revelations" to indicate the manifestations of the divine attributes, but it is clear that it is to be understood in a quite special sense, for the saint plainly distinguishes between these manifestations, which are

[20] *Ascent,* bk. 2, chap. 26.
[21] *Living Flame,* stanza 4.
[22] *Spiritual Canticle,* stanzas 23 and 37.

made in a totally super-conceptual manner, and every other kind of supernatural communications that preserve the distinct and particular mode. He says that these are graces that form "part of the mystical union";[23] they are the prolongation of the higher infused contemplation. Consequently, they are a very different thing from what we are accustomed to term "visions" and "revelations." We conclude that, according to the doctrine of St. John of the Cross, there is no place for particular visions and revelations among the constitutive elements of the higher mystical life.

St. Teresa and St. John of the Cross in Agreement

Do St. Teresa and St. John of the Cross disagree then? It would be a last refuge for a stubborn visionary to be able to declare her preference for St. Teresa. Faced with such a contrast between the two leading lights of mystical theology, she could reject St. John's teaching and invoke an axiom dear to moralists: "A doubtful law is not binding." It would be a triumph for her obstinacy, but we shall drive her out of this last ditch also.

Undoubtedly, the mystical itinerary drawn up by St. John of the Cross is meant to be of general application. He certainly intended to describe the *typical* way of the contemplative soul. This does not mean to say that all the graces that he describes must be verified in an equal manner in all souls that tread the way of contemplation; he even says expressly that there may be more and less, and that he describes the former in order to give us a comprehensive idea of all that may present itself.[24] Yet, trained in the theological schools of his time, St. John accurately distinguishes between what belongs essentially to a state, or a way, and

[23] *Ascent*, bk. 2, chap. 26.
[24] *Spiritual Canticle*, stanza 14, n. 2.

what is added thereto accidentally. He is not content merely to *describe* the Spiritual Marriage; he reveals to us its constitution, its essence, its distinctive features. He is not writing a treatise in Scholastic form, because his object is to *direct*, rather than to *teach*; but in his mind, the concepts are scientifically elaborated, and in his works as a whole, without employing the Scholastic method, he has left us a real theological synthesis of the entire development of the spiritual life. His is a teaching that lays down true *principles* that describe the mystical states in their constituent lines, so that, without much difficulty, we may be able to distinguish what belongs to their essence from what is accidental to them. In a word, as regards the nature of the spiritual journey, St. John gives us a body of teaching that is properly scientific and of universal application.

Can we say as much of the teaching of St. Teresa of Jesus?

I, most certainly, would not wish on any account to lessen the high estimation that the doctrinal eminence of my Mother, St. Teresa, commonly enjoys in the realm of mysticism. I am well aware, also, how highly her philosophical and theological intuition has been exalted. Intuition, however, is not scientific knowledge, and St. Teresa—who was so fond of theologians and knew how to distinguish critically between those who really possessed their theology, such as a Dominic Báñez, her confessor, and certain other half-taught clerics who sometimes led her astray—would be the first to refuse to pose as a theologian. When confronted with the greatest mysteries of the spiritual life, she humbly and joyfully took refuge in her faith in the divine Omnipotence, leaving it to the theologians to examine into the whys and wherefores. "In all these matters, we must stop looking for reasons why they happened; if our understanding cannot grasp them, why should we try to perplex it? It suffices us to know that He who brings this to pass is all-powerful."[25] And elsewhere: "This with all your learning, your Reverences will understand. There is nothing more that I can say of it."[26]

No, St. Teresa had no intention of methodically investigating the *nature* of the supernatural facts. Where, on the other hand, she shows herself an incomparable guide, is in *describing* the mystical facts. Her wonderful capacity for introspection, accompanied by an uncommon facility and clarity in expressing herself, have caused the books wherein she analyzes her personal experiences, both precisely and in a particularly controlled and balanced manner, to be a veritable mine of psychological material of the first order. Mystical theology has been enriched with an abundance of information gained from experience, which has enabled it to state the mystical problem more precisely than hitherto. We must not seek the scientific value of St. Teresa elsewhere than in the field of psychology, and in this field, she is truly *supreme*. But we must also see the consequences of this. The direct value of St. Teresa's descriptions is a documentary one. They are psychological analyses, but *they are not researches into the essence of the matters therein described*. She describes the states and development of the mystical life *as experienced by her*, not directly as the ideal and normal type of the mystical evolution.

Perhaps you will say: That may be true in the case of her autobiography, but it is not verified in *The Interior Castle*, in which she seems to be speaking of contemplative souls in general.

To this difficulty I shall reply with a conclusion that I reached after a detailed study wherein I compared the spiritual progress as related in *The Life of St. Teresa* and in the lengthy *Spiritual Relations*,

[25] *Castle*, Fifth Mansion, chap. 1.
[26] *The Life of St. Teresa of Avila* [hereafter, *Life*], chap. 18.

which constitute a kind of prolongation of that book, with the evolution of the soul as described in *The Interior Castle*. In this latest book, also, especially throughout the mystical portion (i.e., beginning at the Fourth Mansion), St. Teresa is continually describing her own personal experience. The different mansions of the Castle relate her individual progress, with all its personal characteristics; it is a concrete case that is presented as a type – I would rather say, as an example – of the manner in which the mystical evolution of the soul is revealed.

With her facile intuition, St. Teresa also distinguishes, to some extent, what must be considered essential in the graces assigned to the different mansions from what is to be held as adventitious and accidental; but on the whole, directly she is describing her personal experience in its *concrete* form, in which the accidental elements are found together with those that are essential. The very language of the book clearly reveals this method of hers. For instance, when speaking of the vision of the humanity of Our Lord, which accompanies the grace of the Spiritual Marriage, she writes: "To other people the experience will come in a different way. To the person of whom we have been speaking, the Lord showed Himself one day, when she had just received Communion, in great splendour and beauty and majesty, as He did after the Resurrection, and told her that it was time she took upon her His affairs as if they were her own, and that He would take her affairs upon Himself."[27] Evidently the saint is here referring to the grace that she received on November 18, 1572 – and told in number 36 of the *Spiritual Relations* – on which occasion, Our Lord said to her: "As a true wife, be zealous for my honour. My honour is thine and thine is mine." Notice how she also knows that this grace need

---

[27] *Castle*, Seventh Mansion, chap. 2.

not necessarily come under the form of a distinct vision. In fact, she says: "To other people the experience will come in a different way." Why cannot the manifestation of the presence of the Word in the center of the soul, profoundly united to the whole Trinity, suffice? Then we could no longer talk about a vision.

Moreover, on the different occasions when Teresa speaks of visions and revelations, these are always introduced by some expression that marks their adventitious character. The chapter that deals with divine locutions opens with these characteristic words: "There is another way in which God arouses the soul."[28] Hence, locutions are only one way among many of which God may make use. When, a little later, she begins to speak about visions, she again alludes to their accidental character. It happens, she says, that the Lord *sees fit* to reveal to the soul (that is enjoying the intuitive suspension) some secret of His, or some imaginary vision.[29] Therefore, if He does not see fit, the soul will remain deprived of such favors and will receive only the unitive contemplation that constitutes the substance of the rapture. So the precarious character of these extraordinary graces did not escape even St. Teresa, and it is very significant, in this connection, how also, in the book of her *Life*, she has treated *separately* of the development of mystical prayer and of the visions and revelations that she experienced.[30]

I conclude that even if St. Teresa had not remarked upon this adventitious character of the visions, her descriptive method, based on her personal and concrete experience, would forbid us to deduce therefrom a disagreement between her exposition and the doctrine

[28] *Castle*, Sixth Mansion, chap. 3.

[29] *Castle*, Sixth Mansion, chap. 4.

[30] St. Teresa treats of prayer from chapters 11 to 22; from chapter 25, she begins to speak of locutions and visions.

of St. John of the Cross; but since she has frequently noted the accidental character of these graces, we are more than ever in a position to assert her full conformity upon this point with the teaching of the Mystical Doctor.

⌒

Further, we find solid confirmation of this unity of teaching between the two great lights of the Teresian mystical school in the fact that, upon this matter, no divergence can be found among the theologians who proclaim themselves their disciples. All are at one in asserting that visions and revelations are of a distinct order from those graces that belong to contemplative prayer; and while recognizing that the latter are fundamentals in the development of the mystical life, they attribute to the former a very secondary importance.

The Evidence of Facts

To the doctrinal testimony may be added the witness of facts. Besides its two founders, the Teresian Carmel counts two other chosen souls to whom Holy Church has granted the honors of canonization. These are St. Teresa-Margaret of the Sacred Heart, "the Lily of Florence," and St. Thérèse of the Child Jesus, the "Little Flower," who has won the heart of the whole Catholic world. There can be no doubt that these saints lived—in a perfect manner—the Carmelite life to which they were called by God, the lines of which were traced by the two great spiritual leaders of their religious family. Now, during the whole life of St. Teresa-Margaret, there is only one incident to record that can be called a "supernatural locution." When she was still a schoolgirl in the Benedictine monastery of St. Apollonia in Florence, when bidding goodbye to a young girl who was about to enter the convent of the

Discalced Carmelites in that city, she twice heard the voice of St. Teresa distinctly calling her also to be one of her daughters.[31] This fact was considered truly supernatural by two expert directors, but it was quite sporadic in the life of this young saint. For the rest, she was a great contemplative, who knew what it was to be utterly absorbed in God, and she also went through those typical, passive trials of contemplative souls called by St. John of the Cross "the passive Night of the Spirit."

The life of St. Thérèse of the Child Jesus is now known to everybody. In her childhood, she was cured of a serious illness by the miraculous intervention of Our Lady, who showed herself animating, and rendering marvelously beautiful in the child's eyes, the statue before which, together with her sisters, the patient was beseeching God to have mercy upon her. Our Lady smiled, but she did not utter a word.[32] Here, again, we have a single incident. It is true that there was another incident, which the saint called "the prophetic vision," in which, when still a child, she saw in the garden of her home a mysterious figure, in whom she believed she recognized her father, who was one day to be tried by God with a humiliating malady.[33] The nature of this phenomenon is not at all clear, however, and, even if it be considered supernatural, it is only a second incident, and so a very rare occurrence in the childhood of the "little saint." Throughout her subsequent religious life, there is not even one single such fact to relate, yet who can ever sound the depths of spiritual life reached by that

---

[31] Fr. Stanislaus de S. Teresa. *Un Angelo del Carmel*, chap. 5. No modern English biography exists. One was published in 1839 by Sr. Teresa Mary Hartwell, an English Carmelite of the convent in Ronciglione, Italy, and printed by Richardson of London. — Trans.

[32] *Story of a Soul*, chap. 3.

[33] *Story of a Soul*, chap. 2.

saint whose life is generally considered a perfect model for the modern generation?

The evidence of facts, therefore, confirms that of the Teresian doctrine. In the development of the spiritual and mystical life, visions and revelations occupy therein an absolutely secondary and accidental place.

Conclusion

This brief survey of the evolution of the highest spiritual life in the light of Teresian teaching has brought out how absolutely erroneous it is to characterize the mystical life as a life full of visions and revelations. For St. John of the Cross, there is no doubt that even the loftiest states of the contemplative life may be verified without the soul's being endowed with such favors, while, on the contrary, infused contemplation and mystical union constitute the whole substance of the highest form of spiritual life.

It is true that there are mystics who, over and beyond this contemplation, have been favored with special heavenly communications, and among these must be counted St. Teresa of Jesus, the great Mistress of the contemplative life. It may even be said that some over-hasty and superficial reader of her works may think that she makes the higher stages of the mystical life consist in a profusion of such extraordinary graces. Yet we have shown that, bearing in mind her particular method, and accurately examining the actual phraseology of her writings, not only does she not contradict the position of St. John of the Cross, but she also recognizes the accidental character of the phenomena. The Teresian school is unanimous in teaching that these favors are graces of a secondary order, not required for spiritual progress.

Hence, the question arises as to what attitude we should take up toward such graces. Are they to be desired, or are they, perchance, to be despised? Are they useful, or are they, rather, obstacles to the spiritual life? To say that they are accidental is not, indeed, the same thing as to say that they are absurdities. Those who have in mind the ineptitudes in which some devotee relates her meetings with the Child Jesus will rightly shrug their shoulders. But, on the other hand, certain heavenly manifestations met with in the lives of some canonized saints are found to be very interesting. Think, for example, of St. Margaret Mary's relations with the Sacred Heart! Consequently, a more precise knowledge of these phenomena, and their various species and forms, is requisite for one who would answer adequately the question: How ought we to behave in regard to visions and revelations?

For this reason, in the following chapters, we shall try to form a clear and distinct concept of all these extraordinary phenomena, and to give to them a logical classification that will enable us to gain a more concrete idea of the problem that they raise; to distinguish their different aspects, and to treat more definitely of the attitude to be adopted in regard to them.

The rich experience of St. Teresa, which we shall set forth in its concrete form, will supply us with a body of very varying material that will be distinctly coordinated in the light of the principles of St. John of the Cross. The theological analyses of these phenomena will bring out more clearly how many and various are the illusions to which visions are exposed and how delicate and difficult to solve are the questions respecting their authenticity. Under this aspect also, visions are to be distinguished from mystical contemplation!

There is no need to confuse the "mystic" with the "visionary"—certainly not with the false visionary, deluded by his imagination and obstinate in his own opinion! It is a fact that, often, deluded souls do not allow themselves to be moved in the least by those who are trying to lead them back to sound reason. Fully convinced of their relations with God, they can no longer obey even the ecclesiastical authority. Just think! The idea of contradicting communications that have been heard from the lips of God Himself! How rash! The fact is that their follies often throw discredit not only upon revelations, but upon the mystical life itself.

But the latter must never be confused even with true visions. These phenomena are altogether extraordinary in the spiritual life; they do not belong to its normal or usual evolution; they are not even integral elements of the highest states of contemplation and mystical union.

Mystical contemplation, on the contrary, is a mark of a singular fullness of spiritual life, usually granted to the soul that, living a life distinguished by humility and deeply rooted virtue, reaches that perfection of the love of charity that is shown in the complete conformity of the human will with the will of God. Here, and nowhere else, is the center of the spiritual life. Such is the high ideal that the Christian soul may cherish here on Earth: to give itself wholly to God for love and to receive the fullness of His gifts. That is infinitely more precious than the most attractive visions and revelations.

It is the merit of St. John of the Cross that he has expounded in the clearest possible light how visions must not be confused with true mystical life. He puts the latter before us, in all its purity, with all its attractions, accurately distinguished from all subsidiary phenomena; but reaching unto the most intimate union of the Spiritual Marriage, John is the great teacher, revealing to us, in all its completeness, the beauty of the Christian ideal of union with God, even in this world. Grateful for light so great, let us learn to be docile and to obey when he bids us to be prudent with respect to visions and revelations. His care for us is born of his zeal for our welfare. He would not have our spiritual ascent retarded by an unreasonable attachment to secondary graces. He is exacting, but he repays us with security, and he raises the fairest hopes. He opens to us, without obstacles, the road that leads to the loftiest heights; to all-embracing perfection, to the closest union possible between the soul and God.

2

The Problem of Visions and Revelations

"Some people seem to be terrified if they merely hear the words visions and revelations.... For the present, I do not intend to concern myself with distinguishing the good from the bad.... I will only explain how any one should behave who finds herself in such circumstances...."[34]

These few sentences, gathered from a short treatise on visions, inserted by St. Teresa in her *Book of Foundations*, characterize very well the problem that confronts a rather thoughtful soul when, in the course of its spiritual life, these particular phenomena, commonly known as visions and revelations, present themselves.

Ordinarily, the first feeling experienced is a kind of surprise, almost terror; however, the intellectual reaction follows: What ought I to do?

This is the natural attitude of a reasonable being in the face of a new phenomenon that has just intruded itself into his life.

What is it? What is to be done? Two questions: the first speculative, the second practical; but seemingly, closely connected. Indeed, it seems evident that the attitude that we should take up with regard to a thing or a fact depends on its nature. Moreover, the

---

[34] *Book of Foundations* [hereafter, *Foundations*], chap. 8.

practical behavior must be guided by the speculative question. What, however, is not demonstrated is that our *whole* attitude in practice presupposes the *complete* knowledge of the nature of the facts presented to us. This is not always easy to acquire, and often it is attained only after long delays. Shall we, perhaps, be compelled to suspend all action on our part until we have completed our investigation? If such were the case, we should sometimes be in despair!

Fortunately, the existence of principles and general truths permits us to overcome these difficulties. There are certain courses of action that can be shown to be opportune, given any hypothesis whatever; that is to say, they are justified by the general character of the facts that require our reaction. In this case, in order to act, it is not necessary that we should understand the phenomenon before us, even in its most minute details. It is enough to have recognized its general character. May not this be the case with visions and revelations?

There is no denying that human curiosity is easily stimulated by visions. Those who come across such, whether in their own personal lives or in the souls under their direction, easily remain somewhat perplexed. They frequently think that it is highly urgent to pronounce an opinion concerning the nature of the happenings; or more particularly, as to whether the origin of these be human, divine, or diabolic. Hence, they have recourse to rules for the discernment of "true" from "false" visions; often, however, they fail to reach a decision. Or even—and this is much more serious—in their haste to decide, in order to take further action, it happens that they make up their minds without having carefully examined the facts. If this ill-founded opinion be favorable, the door is thrown open to the most serious mistakes.

But is this exactly the first problem that the director of one favored with visions should examine?

St. Teresa does not seem to think so. The small work to which we have referred was written precisely for the instruction of persons whose duty it is to direct the souls entrusted to them. Yet, Teresa writes: "At present, I do not intend to concern myself with distinguishing the good from the bad.... I will say only how she must be guided who finds herself in such circumstances." On the contrary, therefore, the saint turns her attention away from that aspect that is often considered the more urgent. Which is right?

Basing ourselves on the instructions of the great authorities of the Carmel, Sts. Teresa and John of the Cross, we are aiming in this study at showing which is the more important aspect of the problem of visions, as well for the soul who receives them as for the director who has the responsibility of advising that soul. We shall see that, to a great extent, we can disassociate ourselves from the vexed question of the origin of the visions—without in the least hindering the progress of the soul. Rather, in fact, shall we be furthering that in the best possible way.

In order to proceed clearly, however, we must first determine what is to be understood by "visions." Perhaps, we have no personal experience of them, and it is not at all fitting that we should desire such. Consequently, we must have recourse to the experience of others. With this object in view, I do not think that I could suggest a more interesting case, or one better documented, than that of St. Teresa. While, on the one hand, all these graces were particularly abundant in her life, and took on various forms, on the other, her wonderful gift of introspection and her talent for description, joined to an extraordinary simplicity, make us assured that in her writings we possess a true picture of what actually happened.

Visions and Revelations

We shall begin, therefore, by briefly passing in review the different visions and distinct revelations of the saint; then, having classified them in some logical order, we shall relate shortly how she behaved with respect to these graces. When we have completed this informative study, the twofold problem of the qualification of the visions and of the soul's attitude when confronted with these phenomena will have taken on a more clear-cut and concrete form; hence, we shall understand both the difficulty of the former problem and the urgency of the latter.

The Visions of St. Teresa of Jesus

It would seem as though God willed to make of St. Teresa of Jesus the most complete type of the mystical soul. In her, not only do we find all the stages of the so-called contemplation that constitutes the substance of the mystical life — in their most highly developed form — but we could scarcely mention any form of extraordinary grace that she did not know. We intend to describe briefly the classes of these graces, following the order in which they presented themselves in her life.

The First Vision of St. Teresa

St. Teresa of Jesus is not to be reckoned among the saints who were such from the cradle. On the contrary, she was not finally converted until she was nearly forty years of age. She had, notwithstanding, a period of fervor in the early years of her religious life, when she was twenty-two. She gave herself very earnestly to prayer and even reached the stage of having at times the mystical prayer of union. Her piety did not last. She became dissipated, too fond of amusing herself with the visits of her friends, and lost everything.

One day, while she was conversing with a person with whom she would have done better not to associate too frequently, a strange incident occurred. "Christ revealed Himself to me in an attitude of great sternness, and showed me what there was in this that displeased Him. I saw Him with the eyes of the soul—that is, with the imagination—more clearly than I could ever have seen Him with those of the body; and it made such an impression upon me that, although it is now more than twenty-six years ago, I seem to have Him present with me still."[35]

At the time, Teresa was afraid; then, taking note of the fact that the vision was not exterior (it was, in fact, *imaginary*)[36] she began to ponder over the possibility that it existed only in her imagination. Finally, she resumed her conversation.[37] Obviously, she had not benefited much by it! She was then twenty-five.

To find another such incident, we must go to the period of her definitive conversion. This was the effect not of a vision but entirely of reflection. The sight of an impressive statue of the *Ecce Homo*, followed by the reading of St. Augustine's *Confessions*, furnished the occasions.[38] We remain still in the order of means within the reach of all. God was pleased to restore to her, thus converted, mystical prayer, and, knowing her own unworthiness, Teresa lovingly laments her past remissness before Him who had shown her such great mercy. Then, for the first time, she heard an interior voice: "Serve thou me, and meddle not with this."[39] Another moment of fright! But this also remains an isolated incident.

---

[35] *Life*, chap. 7.

[36] The word "imaginary" is here used in its strict psychological sense; there is no suggestion of illusion. —Trans.

[37] *Life*, chap. 7.

[38] *Life*, chap. 9. The statue of the *Ecce Homo* (Behold the Man [John 19:5]) depicted Christ scourged and crowned with thorns. —Ed.

[39] *Life*, chap. 19.

Only two years later—that is, when Teresa was forty-two—did the interior words, the *locutions*, as she calls them, begin to multiply. The first of the series was spoken to her when she was in ecstasy. For some time, she had been struggling hard to detach her heart from certain affections that, even though harmless, did not leave her sufficiently free; but she had not quite succeeded. Then there came the rapture, and she heard: "I will have thee converse now not with men but with angels."[40] From that moment, she felt that her heart was completely detached. Some locutions are very powerful and efficacious.

Supernatural Locutions

Teresa has left an exact description of the phenomenon of locutions. "Though perfectly formed, the words are not heard with the bodily ear; yet they are understood much more clearly than if they were so heard, and however determined one's resistance, it is impossible not to hear them."[41]

We are on the same plane as that of the vision of which we have already spoken. The words do not come from without; they are not heard with the ears; they are interior, *imaginary*. But the phenomenon is quite distinct. The words are "perfectly formed," and "they are understood much more clearly than if heard outwardly"; they even impose themselves; it is impossible *not to hear them*. The phenomenon in question is perfectly clear and the soul feels itself completely passive. If these characteristics were lacking, Teresa would not hold it to be a revelation. She believes, indeed, that such words may be a trick of the fancy; she even warns us that we must not "as soon as the imagination brings something before

[40] *Life*, chap. 24.
[41] *Life*, chap. 25.

34

our mind forthwith think it to be a vision." "Believe me," she says, "when there is question of real visions, we very well know it."[42] Words that are not clear, and in which the mind must intervene in order to make them intelligible, she would simply reject.

Another characteristic of real locutions is that they remain fixed in the memory, and we are unable to forget them. This is especially true in the case of prophetic words that foretell future events. The fact is that locutions may be distinguished from one another according to their objective content. Some are concerned with the spiritual profit of the soul. Such are words of comfort, encouragement, or even reproof. In such cases, the soul is filled with confusion and humility; the reproof goes home, penetrating it to the quick, and is effective; the soul amends. The words of comfort are equally efficacious; forthwith, the soul feels itself strengthened.

Other locutions, again, impose some undertaking upon the soul: an action to be carried out, an admonition, or a counsel to transmit. Since, in such a case, it is a matter of *acting* upon an impulse that is believed to be divine, such a locution must be carefully examined: "When the locution orders us to do something," writes Teresa, "it is necessary to discuss it with a learned and prudent director, and neither to do nor believe anything, save as he tells us."[43]

Lastly, some locutions foretell future events; that is, they are prophetic. Teresa experienced a number of this kind. "These last impress us by their complete certainty.... Even if many years go by, the soul never loses its belief that, in the end, what He has said will come true as, in fact, it does."[44]

---

[42] *Foundations*, chap. 8.
[43] *Foundations*, chap. 8.
[44] *Castle*, Sixth Mansion, chap. 3.

This, their fulfilment, is the most convincing test of their origin. "Sometimes, these locutions tell us of things that are to happen three or four years hence; there have been many of these, and they have all come true without a single exception. From this, it can be seen that they come from God."[45]

To conclude the subject of locutions, we may note that, besides those that are *imaginary*, Teresa distinguishes two other varieties: *exterior* and *intellectual*.

The exterior are those that are heard with the bodily ears. Teresa states explicitly that she has twice experienced such but did not hear the words clearly; they were rather murmurs. Once the locution was divine; on the other occasion it came from the enemy.[46]

Intellectual locutions are manifestations made immediately to the spirit, without passing by the way of words. They happen particularly, according to the saint, when God wills to reveal to the soul "great truths and mysteries." "The soul suddenly finds itself learned, and the mystery of the Most Holy Trinity, together with other lofty things, is so clearly explained to it that there is no theologian with whom it would not have the boldness to contend in defence of the truth of these marvels."[47] Here is how these manifestations take place: 'The Lord introduces into the inmost part of the soul what He wishes the soul to understand, and presents it not by means of images or forms of words.... It is as if food has been introduced into the stomach without our having eaten it, or knowing how it got there; but we know quite well that it is therein."[48]

[45] *Life*, chap. 26.
[46] *Life*, chaps. 31 and 39.
[47] *Life*, chap. 27.
[48] *Life*, chap. 27.

Sometimes, however, the manifestation is intellectual and imaginary at the same time; then, "not only can the words be heard, but much more can be understood than the words themselves convey."[49]

Hence, in St. Teresa's case, we meet with all kinds of locutions: *exterior*, which are heard with the bodily ears; *imaginary*, which are heard with the hearing of the soul; and *intellectual*, which are wordless. We shall now see how the saint distinguishes in like manner between *visions*.

Supernatural "Visions"

In 1569, the Grand Inquisitor Fernando Valdés, published his celebrated *Index Librorum Prohibitorum*, whereby many devotional books in the vernacular were prohibited. St. Teresa, lover of books as she was, felt it keenly to be suddenly deprived of these "good friends" of hers. "I was very sorry, for the reading of some of them gave me pleasure, and I could no longer continue this, as I had them only in the Latin."[50] It was then that Our Lord said to her: "Be not distressed, for I will give thee a living book."[51] This announced the visions, but the saint did not understand that.

Although she had been favored with revelations for about two years, Teresa had not had any visions excepting the single one experienced in her youth. Now she was forty-four and had been familiar with ecstatic prayer for some two years. Here we have the account of what happened to her on a feast of St. Peter :

> Whilst I was at prayer, I saw Christ at my side or, to put it better, I was conscious of Him, for neither with the eyes of the body nor with those of the soul did I see anything.... Being

---

[49] *Castle*, Sixth Mansion.
[50] *Life*, chap. 26.
[51] *Life*, chap. 26.

completely ignorant that visions of this kind could occur, I was at first very much afraid, and did nothing but weep.... All the time Jesus Christ seemed to be beside me, and as this was not an imaginary vision I could not discern in what form. What I felt very clearly was that all the time He was at my right hand, and a witness of everything that I was doing.[52]

The phenomenon is perfectly "particularized": it is a case of an intellectual perception of the presence of Christ in His humanity. This presence is "localized": "at my right hand," states Teresa; but it does not take on any "form." Hence it is that, in her characteristic terminology based on her personal experience, she calls such an apparition "a vision that is not seen." Later, she will call it an *intellectual* vision. Nevertheless, the perception is very clear: "He presents Himself to the soul by a knowledge brighter than the sun.... The soul distinctly sees that Jesus Christ, the Virgin's Son, is present, though He remains unseen. So clear a knowledge is imprinted upon the soul that to doubt it seems quite impossible."[53]

So it seems evident that the intellect passively receives an intelligible object. Yet since this spiritual object is "localized," the phenomenon cannot be considered purely intelligible.

Not only did Our Lord reveal Himself thus; Teresa was to see in the same manner Our Lady, St. Joseph, other saints, departed souls, and even devils.

⁓

There are, however, intellectual visions that, by their very object, transcend the imagination and belong entirely to the intelligible

[52] *Life*, chap. 28.
[53] *Life*, chap. 28.

order. I would also point out that under the single expression "intellectual vision" Teresa understands two kinds of such divine manifestations that differ considerably.

Some are received actually at the time when the soul is raised to the prayer of rapture. "Certain truths concerning the greatness of God remain so firmly in the soul that even if it had not faith, which will tell it who He is and that it is bound to believe that He is God, the soul would adore Him as such from that very moment."[54]

Hence, there are visions that cause the soul to "recognize" God. St. John of the Cross will call them "intuitions of the naked truths regarding God Himself."[55] As we shall see later, these are not visions in the strict sense of the term but are graces of contemplation.

Other visions, called "intellectual," are manifestations of the mysteries of the Faith. St. Teresa enjoyed, in particular, during many years, a continual intellectual vision of the Trinity. "The Three Persons are seen, individually, and yet, by a wonderful kind of knowledge which is given to it, the soul realizes that, most certainly and truly, all these Three Persons are one Substance, and one Power, and one Knowledge, and one God alone; so that what we hold by faith the soul may be said to grasp by sight."[56] We must not think, however, that there is any question of an intuitive vision, for the saint notes expressly that this is a "representation," a "figure of the truth."[57]

Again, in the realm of visions, St. Teresa's experience did not remain confined to the intellectual order. She has mentioned also

[54] *Castle*, Sixth Mansion, chap. 4.

[55] *Ascent*, bk. 2, chap. 26.

[56] *Castle*, Seventh Mansion, chap. 1.

[57] *Castle*, Seventh Mansion, chap. l, and *Spiritual Relations*, no. 16.

two imaginary visions of Our Lord and has described them down to the smallest details.

Seemingly, these began soon after the intellectual visions. The first manifestation of this kind was that of the sacred humanity, which was revealed progressively. "One day, when I was at prayer, the Lord was pleased to reveal to me nothing but His Hands.... A few days later, I also saw that Divine Face.... I realized that His Majesty was leading me according to my natural weakness, for so much glory all at once would have been more than so base and wicked a person could bear."[58]

There is, indeed, a peculiar grandeur about the imaginary visions of Christ with which St. Teresa was favored. It is Christ glorified whom she sees, and she writes in this connection: "There is such beauty about glorified bodies that the glory which illumines them throws all who look upon such supernatural loveliness into confusion.... Even in its whiteness and radiance alone, it exceeds all that we can imagine.... If what I see is an image, it is a living image ... not a dead man, but the living Christ.... Sometimes, He comes with such majesty that no one can doubt that it is the Lord Himself."[59]

Like the imaginary locutions, so also these visions combine in the object a perfect clearness, even a magnificence, and at the same time a character of necessity, as it were of violence: the soul cannot but see them. "It is all the same whether the eyes be closed or open," writes Teresa; "if the Lord is pleased to make us see it, we shall do so, even against our will. There is nothing powerful enough to distract our attention from it, and we can neither resist it nor attain to it by any diligence or care of our own. This I have

---

[58] *Life*, chap. 28.
[59] *Life*, chap. 28.

conclusively proved by experience."[60] Here, therefore, it is a case of complete passivity; any personal initiative is positively excluded. Our Lord makes Himself seen as far as He wills, and the soul cannot see more than He shows it. "There is no possibility of our subtracting from it, or adding to it; if we try to look at any particular part of it, we at once lose the presence of Christ."[61] St. Teresa confides to us, in this connection, a little delusion—I would rather say "feminine weakness"—of her own. "I particularly desired to see the colour of His eyes, and His stature, *in order to describe them* but I have never been sufficiently worthy to see this, nor has it been of any use for me to attempt to do so; if I tried, I lost the vision altogether." Here we see the soul in love, who wants to *describe* the beauty of the Bridegroom! But divine manifestations are reserved territory; desires that are merely creaturely may not enter here; she must be content with what God shows her.

Let us notice also how short a time this vision of Christ lasted; scarcely the twinkling of an eye! "Although He does this so quickly that we might liken the action to a flash of lightning, this most glorious image is so deeply engraven upon the imagination that I do not believe it can possibly disappear until it is seen where it can be enjoyed to all eternity."[62]

Although He is the principal, Christ is not, however, the only object seen by Teresa in imaginary visions. The Blessed Virgin and others appear to her thus, even her spiritual director, Fr. Gratian.[63] Not all the visions are equally impressive in their splendor, nor even so short as is that of Our Lord.

[60] *Life*, chap. 28.
[61] *Life*, chap. 29.
[62] *Castle*, Sixth Mansion.
[63] *Spiritual Relations*, no. 39.

One last point, *and that a very important one*: this imaginary vision is often accompanied by an intellectual one. In that case, both reveal the object in their particular manner. Such is especially the case for the visions of Our Lord. "These two kinds of vision almost invariably occur simultaneously and, as they come in this way, the eyes of the soul see the excellence, the beauty, and the glory of the most holy Humanity; and in the other way which has been described, it is revealed to us that He is God, and how He is all powerful and can do all things, and command all things, and rules all things, and fills all things with His love."[64]

The parallelism between the visions and locutions is therefore perfect. In both alike, there are intellectual and imaginary manifestations, which may be either separate or simultaneous. Besides these, there are exterior manifestations. Teresa had two locutions of this sort, but as to exterior visions, she repeats several times: "These I have never had."[65]

Classification of St. John of the Cross

We have seen how St. Teresa presents us with a detailed classification of visions and locutions. If we compare it with that furnished by St. John of the Cross, we shall understand its significance more exactly.

As spiritual theologians commonly do, the Mystical Doctor teaches that the graces called "visions" and "revelations" take place according to the three orders of human knowledge: that of the intellect, that of the interior senses, and that of the exterior senses; that is to say, they are intellectual, imaginary, and exterior. But the saint

[64] *Life*, chap. 28.
[65] *Life*, chaps. 28 and 30; *Relations*, no. 4; *Castle*, Sixth Mansion, chap. 9.

shows very positively that, whatever may be the order of knowledge whereby a communication is immediately made, it ends always in the intellect.[66] But the mode whereby it reaches the latter is very different in the three cases. When it is a matter of an intellectual communication, the intelligence receives it in a completely passive manner; it neither constructs nor interprets it but only "knows" it. To repeat St. Teresa's figure, it is as though food were in the stomach without our having eaten.[67] Quite different is the case of a communication that passes via the senses, whether exterior or interior. Here we have an object presented to the eyes or to the imagination; the senses, or the imagination "see" but do not "understand"; to understand or judge is the function of the intellect. To fulfill its office, the latter must interpret the object presented to the senses. But then we are going beyond the order of perfect passivity; here the human activity enters in, with all its liability to make mistakes.

Naturally, the case of a communication being received at the same time in the imagination and in the intellect is not excluded; and in such a contingency, we are confronted with those "mixed" cases that St. Teresa has often mentioned equally in connection with visions as with locutions. But per se, an exterior vision is one that is presented to the eyes; an imaginary vision belongs to the imagination only; each is interpreted by the understanding, and the human understanding can err.

Besides this first reason, which shows how there is a greater possibility of error in external and imaginary visions, there is another that is recognized by all mystical theologians. These visions may come not only from God but also from the devil or from the subject himself. St. Teresa knew from experience counterfeit visions, as also

[66] *Ascent*, bk. 2, chap. 10.
[67] *Life*, chap. 27.

counterfeit locutions. In fact, she tries to determine the criteria whereby we may differentiate between divine locutions and those that are "words which the spirit litters to itself."[68] As for the devil, she declares explicitly, "Three or four times, he has attempted to present the Lord to me by making a false likeness of Him."[69] But she detected the fraud through the evil effects of the vision.

Theology teaches that the devil is able to act upon our sensitive powers and hence to present an object to the understanding by their means. He cannot act directly upon the understanding itself; this region is reserved to God. As for the power of deception possessed by one's own spirit, Teresa had already perceived how great it was. Modern studies in psychiatry, far from restricting her opinion, tend on the contrary rather to extend the danger zone.

Opposition of St. Teresa's Directors

These possibilities of delusion explain why St. Teresa met with such strong opposition from her spiritual directors when she began to receive these favors.

Having described her visions, it will be well to say a word also concerning the attitude that her confessors took up with respect to these graces. It would be hard to find in hagiography a case that was submitted to more opinions and subjected to more discussion than was that of the saint. Yet we shall see how, after many differences of opinion, her visions acted favorably upon and even set the crown upon her spiritual and mystical life.

As she remarks herself, God led her by the way of fear; and not only God but nearly all her early directors! When, shortly after her conversion, God gave her back the grace of mystical prayer, her

[68] *Life*, chap. 25.
[69] *Life*, chap. 28.

spiritually minded friends considered that she was being deceived by the evil one. There was only one remedy, so they said, and that was for her to submit herself to the direction of the Fathers of the Society of Jesus. Albeit they recognized her good spirit immediately, the Jesuit Fathers kept her under the strictest discipline and laid upon her the command to resist the divine favors. St. Francis Borgia set her free from this, but when the locutions began, there was a veritable war declared. To test the saint, her confessor, Fr. Balthasar Alvarez, gave ear to the fears of Teresa's friends, and, for more than two years, she found herself compelled to join these latter in a real crusade of prayers in order to obtain from God the favor of being led by another way. It was all of no avail. "He continued to speak to me, and that very often."[70]

Nor was this all. Visions were added to the locutions, and then the opposition reached its climax. In the absence of Father Balthasar Alvarez, a confessor went so far as to order the saint to make a contemptuous gesture at the apparition of Our Lord. With great sorrow of heart, but humble and obedient, Teresa obeyed the order received; and then "the Lord told me not to worry about it; that I was quite right to obey, and that He would see that my confessor learned the truth."[71] God sent to Ávila St. Peter of Alcantara, who set the saint's mind at rest and made her friends and confessors understand "and put reasons and arguments before them as to why they should be reassured and leave me in peace."[72]

Teresa had lost nothing by obeying; the grace had remained and increased, and now she could rest tranquilly, assured that the Spirit of God was working in her.

[70] *Life*, chap. 27.
[71] *Life*, chap. 29.
[72] *Life*, chap. 30.

It was the beginning of 1680. The same year, she conceived her plan of the Reform. Visions and locutions, which had hitherto been concerned solely with her personal life, changed their function and now began to counsel her.

Yet, when it was a question of obtaining permission from her superior to carry out an order received in a locution, Teresa made no allusion to the divine communication.[73] The superior was to decide for himself. But personally, the saint found great help therein. "If the Lord had not bestowed on me the favours He has, I think I should not have had the courage to perform the works I have," Teresa wrote some years later. "And so, since beginning my foundations, I have lost the fears which had previously troubled me, when I thought I was suffering from delusions, and I have become certain that it was all the will of God."[74]

Yet, whilst the divine intervention directed her work, visions ever more sublime accompanied her interior life, enabling her to comprehend its utmost depths. The development of mystical love was rendered, as it were, palpable through the increasing intimacy shown her by the apparitions of Our Lord and His bearing toward her. Then He introduced her into the communion of the Father and even into the very heart of the Trinity, and when Teresa attained to the Spiritual Marriage, wherein the soul experiences a certain participation in the Trinitarian life and a kind of vital identification with Christ, she "saw" the Trinity, whose life she shared; and she "saw" Jesus, to whom she was so closely united.[75]

The opposition that St. Teresa encountered on the part of her confessors did not hinder in the least the work that God willed to

[73] *Life*, chap. 32.
[74] *Spiritual Relations*, no. 34.
[75] *Castle*, Seventh Mansion, chaps. 1 and 2.

accomplish in her by means of the visions. It even rather served to render her quite sure as to the divine origin of these favors and to preserve her from all delusion. Under the rigid discipline imposed upon her, Teresa entered into peaceful possession of the highest charismata, as well as that of an incomparably profound mystical life.

The Twofold Problem of Visions

The study of St. Teresa's case has, I think, given a more precise sense to the questions that we spontaneously put to ourselves when visions are in question. Evidently, to determine their nature constitutes a complex problem. It is necessary to distinguish the quality of the phenomenon—that is, to ascertain whether we are dealing with an external, imaginary, or intellectual vision; then to decide as to its origin, whether divine, diabolical, or merely human. Neither of these questions can be answered without serious difficulties.

We know already that intellectual visions are much less liable to error than those that are imaginary or external; but it is not easy to be sure whether we are really dealing with an intellectual vision. Let the director be on his guard, moreover, not to let it be seen that he is more inclined to credit intellectual visions than the other sorts! Otherwise, I think, all his penitents will tell him that their visions are intellectual! Nor again, is it very easy for a person who has not at least a little philosophical knowledge to distinguish a purely intellectual phenomenon from one that is imaginary, or accompanied by some schematic imagery. And not all have a gift of introspection and analysis comparable to that of St. Teresa. Often the director has to be content with inadequate replies, and he must also beware lest he himself suggest the replies in his questions. Such a proceeding would be simply an illusion. Moreover, it would seem that purely intellectual visions are much less frequent than the others. Hence it comes about that, practically speaking, the director must consider the occurrence as belonging, at least in part, to the sensible order. But forthwith, he is faced with the other problem in all its difficulty: that of the origin of the vision. Has he to deal with a vision of divine origin?

What Is a "Divine" Vision?

And, first of all, what do we understand by a vision of divine origin?

This depends, naturally, on the idea we have of the psychological structure, or "mechanism" of visions. Therefore, we must necessarily examine to some extent the philosophical-theological problem of the nature of visions, taking as typical those that are imaginary and those met with most frequently. Only after this examination shall we be able to say precisely what we intend to attribute to God in a vision, when we pronounce it "divine."

In this connection, I would like to remark that some mystical writers too readily assimilate the internal structure of visions *in genere* to that of a prophetic vision, or a revelation.

In the latter, St. Thomas Aquinas distinguishes a double element: a sensible presentation of the object, and an infused, charismatic light whereby, the saint teaches, the soul knows with certainty the object revealed and also remains convinced of the divine origin of the manifestation.[76] This light is the substantial element of the prophetic charisma. Its intervention is necessary precisely because, in prophecy, the intellect knows a truth that it could not possibly learn without a directly divine manifestation. Prophetic knowledge is preternatural, miraculous. St. John of the

---

[76] *Summa Theologica*, II-II, q. 171, art. 5; *Contra Gentiles* bk. 3, chap. 154.

Cross admits that, now also, such visions still exist,[77] but we must not put them all on the same level.

Not all visions have an object so exalted that it cannot be known without the intervention of a charismatic light; hence, that must not be considered a constitutive element of every vision on this account. St. Thomas even points out expressly that sometimes there may be a sensible presentation without the charismatic light. And speaking of such a case, he adds that such a sensible presentation "is something imperfect in the genus of prophecy."[78]

We have seen above that, for St. John of the Cross, imaginary visions are nothing else per se than a sensible presentation of the object, whereof the intellect judges. From this we may conclude that such visions and locutions are definitely imperfect divine manifestations.

We must, however, go further and examine also in what exactly the sensible manifestation itself may be called divine. Must we think necessarily of a preternatural intervention, in some way miraculous? We may here note that St. Thomas, even while affirming *in genere* that in the prophetic vision there is conferred on the human mind something that surpasses the natural faculty[79]—and this even in the sensible presentation—restricts this divine intervention, in certain cases, to a simple arranging of the sensible, natural species.[80]

---

[77] *Ascent*, bk. 2, chap. 26.

[78] *Summa Theologica*, II-II, q. 171, art. 5.

[79] "Now the gift of prophecy confers on the human mind something which surpasses the natural faculty." *Summa Theologica*, II-II, q. 173, art. 2.

[80] "By means of imaginary forms, either of exclusively Divine origin and not received through the senses ... or divinely coordinated from those derived from the senses." *Summa Theologica*, II-II, q. 173, art. 2.

Visions and Revelations

When it is a question of a vision of Christ glorified, as we have
seen in the case of St. Teresa, we might readily suppose that the
natural species do not suffice. If, on the other hand, the apparition
has not this character of transcendent beauty, or if it be only a
matter of certain words heard in the imagination, we no longer see
the necessity for such higher intervention; we may more probably
remain in the natural order; we might even ask ourselves whether
it be rightly necessary to go outside of it. Might we not think that
the psychological mechanism of such visions is simply natural? I
would not venture to assert it as proved at present, but I do not
wish to hide the fact that, among some Catholic psychologists
enjoying an excellent reputation, there exists a tendency to identify
the psychological mechanism of certain exterior and imaginary
visions with that which intervenes in sensorial and psychic hallucinations.[81] Do not be scandalized! There is no question of
identifying visions and hallucinations. We wish to say solely that,
in both cases, the presentation of the sensible object may be the
work of the same psychological mechanism; but the cause that
sets the mechanism in motion is completely different. Whereas,
in hallucination, this mechanism operates under the influence
of morbid conditions, in visions it is moved by the influence of
the operating grace.

[81] "There are first sensible, corporal visions, the psychological mechanism of which enters necessarily into the framework alike of sensa-
tion and hallucination.... We should be inclined to say the same
as regards imaginary visions.... The psychological mechanism of
these imaginary visions offers nothing that distinguishes them
fundamentally from pseudo-hallucinations, with or without precise
spatial presentation of the image." Joseph Maréchal, S.J., *Études
sur la psychologie des mystiques*, 2nd éd. (Paris: Desclée De Brouwer,
1938), 125–127.

In confirmation of their theories, these writers point out that even in the simply natural order, there are phenomena of hallucinatory form that are quite other than morbid and even scientifically fruitful. They cite as an instance the case of the chemist Kekulé, who, after having been long absorbed in searching for the structural formula of benzine, became drowsy and, in that condition, had a hypnogogic hallucination that showed him, schematically, the solution of his problem. The atoms began to dance before his eyes, to arrange themselves finally in the circular form of a serpent biting its own tail. Under the influence of his vision, the chemist resumed his study and, some hours later, the celebrated "benzine hexagon" was born.[82] If the hallucinatory mechanism can intervene in a useful scientific manner, why should it not intervene in an analogous way in the spiritual life?

I do not wish to claim that we should consider the thesis as completely demonstrated, but it cannot be denied that its positions are worthy of serious attention. We should, at least, deduce therefrom that it is not enough to have recognized the influence of the spirit of God in a vision in order to be able to conclude immediately that we are faced with a preternatural, miraculous, divine intervention. Certainly, this preternatural intervention is not to be excluded a priori, even in cases of sensible visions, but it is probable that there may exist a sensible, divine vision of which the mechanism would be natural, and only the impulsion of the divine, operating grace that moves this mechanism be supernatural. In this case, we should have a *divine-natural* vision, and so, in fact,

---

[82] "There may be visions that semiologically are only hallucinations and nevertheless have a real religious value." Roland Dalbiez, "Marie-Thérèse Noblet considérée du point du vue psychologique," *Études carmélitaines* 23 (October 1938): 22.

these writers name such. We may grant that such a vision does belong to the *supernatural order* (and therefore, it may be said to be divine) but not to that which is *preternatural* (and therefore, it may be said to be natural).

It is understandable that in such a vision the personal stamp of the soul that receives it may be very deep, and it would be a gross error to consider everything as though it had simply "fallen from Heaven." We shall see later how these considerations throw much light on the interpretation of some revelations, too easily believed to be words "out of the mouth of God"![83] All the more are we convinced that, be it only in order to determine clearly what precisely we understand by the divine element of a vision, the qualification of revelations presents a very delicate problem. In short, we are going to end by finding ourselves deep in religious psychology, without having reached positions that are completely demonstrable, however interesting they may be.

Add to this first difficulty that of the use of the criteria commonly indicated by spiritual writers whereby we may recognize the divine influence in a vision—and this, also, is no easy problem, but we reserve it to another chapter—and I think you will be of opinion that, in order to be able to get to the bottom of the question of the qualification of visions, one needs to be a specialist and know how to employ all the resources of theology and religious psychology.

The More Urgent Problem

Must we conclude, therefore, that every spiritual director who is not a specialist in such matters must perforce hand over to someone else every penitent of his who is favored with visions?

---

[83] *Ascent*, bk. 2, chap. 29.

I am sure that such a conclusion would seem exaggerated to everyone, and the fact is that such is not the case. But we must show also why this is so.

Let us return, for a moment, to the two questions that the confessor, as well as the penitent, spontaneously asks himself when a soul under his care appears to have visions: What is it? What is to be done?

Obviously, he cannot wait to act until he has answered the first query. Now that we know all the difficulties involved, it is certain that, without a meticulous searching into the matter, he will not reach any satisfactory solution. Meanwhile, must he leave everything as it is and abandon the soul to its impressions? That is not permissible. Certainly St. Teresa's directors did not think so, seeing that they gave her practical guidance before they were able to judge of the nature of her visions, and yet that guidance was shown to be very profitable. There must be a safe attitude that we can take up from the first, an attitude that can be known sufficiently, independently of a question so abstruse as is that of determining the nature of the visions.

It is understood, however, that teaching such as will meet the facts must find its justification in the general principles that must govern the spiritual life. But is not this, perhaps, the fundamental task of a good director: namely, to apply these principles to all the various events of the spiritual life, so as to procure in everything the greater progress of the soul in holiness and union with God?

The science properly belonging to and characteristic of the director is spiritual theology, which has for its object *the acquiring of perfection*. Hence, for the spiritual father, the fundamental question, dominating all others in his relations with his spiritual children, is that of their progress in union with God. Everything that he must examine in souls presents itself to him under the fundamental aspect of their spiritual welfare. Even visions and revelations are of interest to him only insofar as they may promote or retard souls in the way of perfection. Consequently, the aspect of these phenomena that formally interests the director is evidently that of the use that we must make of them in order to derive the greatest possible profit therefrom.

This is the reason why, even while he is treating at length of visions, St. John of the Cross states that his intention in so doing is "the direction of the soul, through all its apprehensions, natural and supernatural ... to divine union with God."[84] For the Mystical Doctor, also, it is not the qualifying of the visions—that is to say, the study of their nature, their psychological structure—that is the primary concern of the director but, rather, the problem of the attitude that should be assumed with respect to these phenomena.

Certainly, we should not be uninterested in the problem of their qualification because this also belongs to the problem in its entirety, and the said problem is not adequately disposed of until we have answered the very difficult question of their origin and structure; but the spiritual director has not to solve it, save insofar as it is necessary to enable him to decide upon the attitude that he should take up. In the measure in which he can base his attitude solidly upon other principles than those of the accurate determination of the nature of these occurrences, he may also put off this examination to a more convenient season, even sometimes omit it altogether.

We conclude that the problem of determining the nature of the vision enters only secondarily into spiritual theology and is subsidiary to that of the attitude of the soul; it belongs directly to the field of religious psychology, albeit enlightened by theological

---

[84] *Ascent*, bk. 2, chap. 28, no. 1.

principles. On the contrary, the question of the attitude to be adopted, alike by the director and the penitent, when confronted with these extraordinary phenomena of the supernatural life, belongs directly and per se to the science of spiritual direction—that is, to *spiritual theology*.

⁀

In this *spiritual* problem of visions, we may distinguish two aspects: the first general, the second particular. It is indeed useful to determine how far visions *in genere* are bound up with the development of the spiritual and mystical life. It is the question we examined in the first chapter of this book. Taking our stand upon the teaching of St. Teresa and St. John of the Cross, we have come to the conclusion that, in the spiritual life, visions are entirely accidental phenomena, without which it is possible to attain to the highest mystical contemplation.

It remains now to examine two matters that more directly concern the manner of comporting ourselves in face of the fact of the visions: first, that of the attitude that the soul must assume, and that the director must teach it, and second, that of the director's manner of proceeding. This will be the object of the two following chapters.

Conclusion

We have now entered fully into the heart of the arduous and complex problem of visions.

We now know clearly what we must understand by visions and locutions. St. Teresa's precise descriptions have revealed to us a whole world of interesting and reliable facts, distributed over three planes: the external, the imaginary, and the intellectual.

We have also a more detailed knowledge of the different problems to which the existence of these facts gives rise in a reasonable soul that desires to walk securely in spiritual ways and not expose itself to becoming the plaything of its fancy. We may state them in two words: "qualification" and "attitude."

The matter of qualification or, more precisely, of the origin and structure of the visions, is, as we have seen, complicated, delicate, and difficult.

Fortunately, however, this has been shown to be not the most urgent question for the spiritual director. His concern is more directly that of the attitude to be assumed toward the visions, in order to derive from them the greatest possible profit. In this, we have recognized the real spiritual problem of the visions, which belongs directly to ascetic and mystical theology.

We do not hide the fact that this, also, has its difficulties. But we face them confidently, relying on the teaching of a master whose writings are full of heavenly wisdom. On the spiritual problem raised by visions, we shall follow the teaching of St. John of the Cross. Not blindly, however! He does not ask us to make an act of faith, but he justifies his positions theologically. To profit by his doctrine in order to direct our researches is not at all humiliating; it is an honor to listen to the teaching of a master mind, and in mystical science, Holy Church herself has named him Master and Doctor. With such a guide, we are sure of reaching a right conclusion.

To our confidence we add a hope: that of freeing spiritual direction, up to a point, from a worrying and difficult problem.

By concentrating our attention on the spiritual aspect of this problem of visions, and putting off until another time the task of discerning between the good and the bad, St. Teresa has shown us that the latter matter need not be considered very urgent. When speaking of external visions, St. John of the Cross states more decidedly that the soul must fly from them absolutely, without even wishing to examine whether they be good or bad.[85] So it does not seem that the whole attitude of director or directed, with respect to visions, must be founded on the very difficult task of examining into their origin or their quality.

It is true that if this were requisite for fulfilling his duties, the director ought not to shrink from even the most delicate problems but should face these bravely, trusting in God. But it is not less true that he need not involve himself in difficulties when it is possible to avoid them. Moreover, if spiritual direction were too onerous and complicated a task, many good priests would be afraid to undertake it, and the result would be gravely detrimental to souls. It is fitting, therefore, that we should examine how far the director should enter into the discernment of visions.

If, following the guidance of St. John of the Cross, we succeed in demonstrating that, in order to carry out the duties of his delicate office, the confessor should take his stand upon the general principles of the spiritual life, rather than upon particular analyses of the visions, we shall have effectively lightened, by a considerable weight, the task and responsibility of the guide of souls.

---

[85] *Ascent*, bk. 2, chap. 11, no. 2.

3

"Do Not Receive Them"

In the preceding chapter, we distinguished a twofold problem with respect to visions: that of their *qualification* and that of the *attitude* of the soul in regard to them; and we recognized that it is the latter that directly concerns spiritual theology. That is not to say that we hold a priori that it is independent of the former; we even acknowledge that the question of this dependence must be cleared up and decided if we would reach a doctrine for spiritual direction that is quite safe. But the problem to be faced in the first place is that of the attitude to be assumed.

Now when, as we have announced we mean to do, we seek guidance for our study in St. John of the Cross, we shall not surprise anyone by saying that the problem that he has examined is the *spiritual* one. It is a fact that the object of all his writings is just to lead souls to the closest union with God possible in this world.[86] All the different aspects of the spiritual life of which he treats are always considered from this special standpoint of their relation with the divine union, which is the end to which the soul is tending. This is true also of visions, to which the saint devoted several chapters in his works, especially in the *Ascent of Mount*

---

[86] *Ascent*, prologue.

Carmel. He even states expressly that he does not intend to treat of the subject, saving only in order to instruct the soul and lead it, beyond these, to divine union.[87]

Hence, seemingly, St. John also does not think it necessary to have an exhaustive knowledge of the nature of visions, and their origin, in order to take up the correct attitude toward them.

It does not require a prolonged acquaintance with the works of St. John of the Cross to perceive that he is far from being a friend to visions. His general attitude to such is frankly *negative.*

One day, the superior of a convent confided to me that she was afraid to see her nuns reading the works of St. John of the Cross. "He talks so much about visions and other extraordinary graces," she told me, "that I am frightened lest he should rather turn my daughters' heads!" The good Sister little thought that her words supplied me with the most palpable proof that she had never read the works of St. John of the Cross. It is a fact that he does talk much about visions and revelations but not to recommend them or make his readers desire them. Quite the contrary! While he teaches us to distinguish all these things from the contemplation of living faith, which he is always recommending, as the most efficacious means of leading us to divine union, he is continually repeating, and in every key, with respect to all these particular graces: *No admitir* — do not receive them. We must not receive them; we must renounce them; we must reject them.

So insistent is he that this fact has given rise, in some cases, to another mistaken idea — namely, that the saint condemns all visions absolutely and does not admit that there may be any of which the

[87] *Ascent,* bk. 2, chap. 21.

soul can take account. St. John never falls into such an extremist position. Rather, as the first point of our study will make clear, he has frankly recognized that visions can have a proper place in the spiritual life of the soul. We shall state subsequently the nature of his negative attitude and explain the reasons that justify it, while determining precisely how it should be understood in different cases.

Visions as Means in the Spiritual Life

An overly rigid attitude has also been attributed to St. John of the Cross on other matters of his doctrine. The name of "Doctor of the Absolute," by which he is sometimes called, and which alludes to the quasi-metaphysical form presented by his teaching concerning the way that leads to divine union, has occasionally caused the delicate psychology wherewith he knows how to apply his principles to the differing cases presented by our human life, with all its variety of circumstances, to be neglected. It is but too true also that the celebrated doctrine of the *Nothing* that leads to the *All*[88]—the verses that sum it up have been called "the Canticle of the Absolute"—has been interpreted at times in a sense that is obviously exaggerated, as though St. John wished not merely to reform and cure our damaged sense life but had set himself to crush it out by a kind of systematic repression. It is true that he teaches that the disciplining of the senses and passions, which he proposes, must be undertaken resolutely—that is, energetically and with the aim of subjugating them to the will—but in the same place, he adds that all must be done with order and discretion.[89] He had always a profound sense of the harmony wherewith the work of sanctification adapts itself to human nature. *Gratia non*

[88] *Ascent*, bk. 1, chap. 13.
[89] *Ascent*, bk. 1, chap. 13.

destruit naturam, sed sanat et elevat. "Grace does not destroy nature but heals and elevates."

Even when he wishes to explain how God sometimes makes use of visions in order to promote the holiness of a soul, he bases his teaching on an axiom of St. Thomas that emphasizes the harmonious adaptation of the action of Providence to our human nature: *Deus omnia movet secundum modum eorum.*[90] "God moves all things according to their way."

Just because man possesses a nature composed of sense and spirit, in such wise that the life of his intellect is dependent on that of his senses, so also in the "spiritualizing" of his human nature, the divine action will normally pass by way of the senses before reaching the depths of the perfect spirituality.

Is it not, perhaps, true that in the first spiritual exercises, whereby a soul sets out to seek God, the senses play a notable part? The saint instances explicitly: "to hear Masses, sermons, to see sacred objects, to mortify the taste in food, to chastise the body by penances and holy austerity."[91] But anon, he adds: 'When these senses are to some extent prepared, He is wont to perfect them still further, by bestowing upon them certain supernatural favours and gifts ... such as visions of heavenly things ... sweet perfumes, locutions ..."[92] Likewise, on the plane of the imagination, the soul proceeds to treat with God by the use of meditation, in which it makes use of imaginary representations of holy things. And again, St. John adds: "And when the interior senses are prepared by this natural experience, God is wont to enlighten

[90] *Ascent*, bk. 2, chap. 17.
[91] *Ascent*, bk. 2, chap. 17.
[92] *Ascent*, bk. 2, chap. 17.

and spiritualize them still more by some imaginary visions which are called supernatural."[93]

There can be no doubt but that he recognizes that, at times, the origin of even exterior and imaginary visions that are presented to the soul is to be found in the divine action.

"Well and good" will, perhaps, be the retort of one prone to interpret the saint's teaching too absolutely. St. John grants that there are true visions, but he teaches us to repel them and keep our eyes closed; so it is all the same as if there were none such!

It cannot be maintained that even this is the real sense of his doctrine. He does, indeed, admit that there are cases, rare, it is true, but nevertheless existing, in which we may take account of a communication thus received. He has even expressly stated in connection with those lower types that are made to the exterior senses: 'The soul must take care never to receive these apprehensions, save occasionally and on the advice of a competent person; and even then, it must have no desire for them."[94] The text is clear enough and shows that the saint occasionally limits his general principle of *No admitir.*

Elsewhere, speaking of locutions, he says similarly: "And let it be clearly noted that a soul should never act according to its own opinion, or accept anything of what these locutions express, without much reflection and *without taking advice of another."*[95] Once more, the saint hands the soul over to another's judgment. On this condition, however, he admits that there are cases in which one may give credit to a locution that seems to be supernatural. Hence, his teaching seems to be much less absolute than might

[93] *Ascent*, bk. 2, chap. 17.
[94] *Ascent*, bk. 2, chap. 11.
[95] *Ascent*, bk. 2, chap. 30.

be thought at first sight. On this account, we wish to examine it carefully, in order to decide precisely what he means.

To put it shortly: What does St. John claim to teach with his celebrated *No admitir?*

He teaches us that when confronted with visions, we should take up a strictly negative attitude. That means we are not to cultivate any particular esteem for them, or consider them as favors that are very important for our progress; we are not to desire to have them ourselves or to delight in them when they occur. On the contrary, we must desire never to encounter them throughout our spiritual pilgrimage and must even endeavor to avoid them as far as possible. If, by chance, we are favored with them, we must try to pay no attention to them.

The saint is constrained to show himself so averse to these extraordinary favors for two reasons: the danger lest we become *attached* to visions, to the great detriment of our progress in the way of faith, which alone can unite our mind directly to God; and the danger of our being deluded, owing to the multiple occasions of error furnished.

We shall first explain these two motives on which St. John insists, in order subsequently to come down to the practical matter of how we should behave in consequence. We shall see how his motto *No admitir* admits of many delicate lights and shades when it is applied to concrete cases.

Motives for Rejecting Visions

St. John of the Cross is the Doctor of the union of love between the soul and God. In all his works, his only object is to teach the soul the way there and make it realize the greatness of the end to which it is tending. Wholly preoccupied with "the one thing necessary," it is from this lofty standpoint that he considers the entire organization of the spiritual life. To point out to the soul the means that lead there most directly, to teach it not to waste its time and strength in trifles that will retard the attainment of this union with God: such is the aim of the Mystical Doctor.

In the light of this end to be reached, he has laid down the principles that dominate his entire work: "The soul is not united to God in this life through understanding, nor through enjoyment, nor through the imagination, nor through any sense whatsoever; but only through faith according to the understanding, and through hope according to the memory, and through love according to the will."[96] Or, to put it more briefly, the three theological virtues (inseparable, moreover, from grace, from the other virtues and from the gifts of the Holy Ghost) are the immediate means of our union with God. In fact, the theological virtues constitute the bond between the soul and its supernatural end; they have for their object God Himself, considered in His deity. Consequently, their development unites us ever more closely to Him. Acts of our life of religion, on the other hand, that have a lower object cannot unite our spirit immediately with God. Visions and revelations have as their object things pertaining to our life of religion, granted, but they are things that, for the most part, belong to the created order. They confront us with attractive apparitions, words that move us, and so forth, but all that is not God! Visions are merely an intermediate means of union; so far as the intellect is concerned, union is reserved to faith!

In our book *Acquired Contemplation*,[97] we have shown how St. John does not wish the soul to be attached to distinct concepts of meditation but to know how to surrender itself when God calls it to the contemplation of obscure and loving faith. It must

---

[96] *Ascent*, bk. 2, chap. 6.

[97] See Fr. Gabriel of St. Mary Magdalen, O.C.D., *St. John of the Cross: Doctor of Divine Love and Acquired Contemplation*.

not be troubled when God leads it into the purifying aridity that renders meditation impossible. Another manner of knowing God, much richer than that in which it made use of distinct concepts, humanly elaborated, is substituted for meditation. The soul learns to practice the nobler, more "unitive," act of faith: that in which it turns its gaze immediately to the incomprehensible Godhead itself, which constitutes its proper and formal object. To hinder the development of this gaze of faith in the soul by wishing to return forcibly to the attractive ideas of the meditation would be absurd. It is not distinct concepts that unite us immediately to God but the gaze of obscure faith that, even though guided by the concepts, soars above them to contemplate the divine incomprehensibility.

St. John applies this doctrine to visions and revelations. Even if they do come from God, visions ordinarily have as their object a created being or some particular truth; hence, they are distinct, limited objects of knowledge; they do not attain the height of the formal object of faith; they do not put us into contact with the Godhead itself. To be fond of them, to cling to them, is out of order. Yet the soul does cling to them, all too easily. If it does not abandon the concepts of meditation without difficulty in order to enter into the contemplation of obscure faith, much more easily does it become attached to those thoughts that, as it thinks, come from above. Believing that it has found in visions direct communication with God, it feels inclined to base its whole spiritual life upon them. To do so would be a very serious mistake. Not visions but the theological virtues lead us immediately to union. We may even say that souls that cling to visions thereby hinder their faith from developing and delay their progress on the way to union. The soul that concentrates its attention upon attractive apparitions that may manifest themselves, or that "immerses" itself in the teaching that it thinks it is receiving from the mouth of God, does not keep its mind free to seek God in naked faith. Its affection for the phenomena arouses in it many desires and preoccupations incompatible with the tranquil and serene attitude that prepares our minds for union with God. "For the understanding to be prepared for this divine union, it must be pure and void of all that pertains to sense, and detached and free from all that can be clearly perceived by the understanding, profoundly hushed and put to silence, and leaning upon faith."[98]

Hence, the first motive for forbidding all affection for visions, all willingness to give them any place of importance in our lives, arises out of the very conditions of our preparation for union with God. To be attached to visions and to be properly prepared for divine union are two incompatible states. He who nourishes his spirit upon visions does not nourish it upon faith; and faith alone is the proximate means of union. Visions are but secondary means, of no permanent utility. For this reason, we must permanently relegate them to an inferior place.

Dangers of Error

But that is not enough!

Not only are visions dangerous because they cause us to deviate from the path of faith and waste our time over secondary matters, but they may also lead us into error in many ways.

In the previous chapter, we considered the difficulty presented by the origin of visions. We shall now see how the saint advises the greatest reserve in giving credit to visions just on account of this very difficulty. We shall indeed find some good soul who, even while granting that in the spiritual life visions are only of secondary

[98] *Ascent*, bk. 2, chap. 9.

importance, will think it strange that anyone can possibly advise that they be rejected. Even though they be but remote means of union, they are always thoughts sent from Heaven! How could we fail to receive them with joy and gratitude? If we do otherwise, are we not resisting God Himself?

To this St. John replies: "How do you know that they come from God?" They may, in fact, come from other sources, as St. Teresa also has testified from her experience. There is the devil; there is our personal, subjective condition, the creative power of which it is not so easy to fathom. It is true that there are certain criteria that allow us to investigate the origin of these apparently supernatural communications, but they are difficult to apply, and the conclusions to which they lead are often very limited, amounting to no more than probabilities. This is especially true in the cases of exterior and imaginary visions, which are exposed to many risks of being counterfeited. We know that the influence of the devil may act directly on our sensitive powers, but often there is not even any need to have recourse to him in order to explain certain apparitions. It is not impossible that such are due to sensory hallucinations. The fact that the object may take on the face of a saint makes no change whatever in the substance of the phenomenon. Hallucinations of sacred objects may very well exist. Even the pathological condition known as psychic hallucination, in which certain objects or words are imposed upon the imagination of the subject without the latter's being able to rid himself of them, is a phenomenon that has several points of contact with the imaginary vision.[99] We may sometimes mistake the one for the other.

[99] J. Lhermitte, "Origine et mécanisme des hallucinations," *Études carmélitaines* (April 1933); 111; Pierre Quercy, *L'Hallucination*, vol. 1 (Paris: Felix Alcan, 1930), 287-288.

In confirmation of this, I recall the case, published some years ago in a well-known ascetic review[100] of a good and pious woman, whose life showed no evidence of psychological disturbances and who, on several occasions, heard a voice suggesting certain spiritual counsels that, even though quite unexpected, fitted perfectly and thoroughly into her life. The party who related the incident appeared to favor a divine origin of these locutions. On the other hand, a professor of the Sorbonne, a specialist in psychic maladies, and an excellent Catholic to boot, held the contrary opinion, and even while praising the precision of the observations made by the other, found grounds in those very observations for believing that the occurrence was pathological.[101] If even specialists find it so difficult to decide with certainty, how much harder will it be for one who is no expert to do so!

Purely intellectual communications are less exposed to deception because it is not easy to counterfeit them, at least when the phenomenon remains completely passive, but it is very difficult to be fully certain that our natural spontaneity does not enter in by giving the communication a personal interpretation. And, as we have already said, many persons are incapable of judging concerning the intellectual quality of a phenomenon.

Consequently, visions and revelations constitute a very insecure department, where we must proceed only while taking the strictest precautions. Anyone who is determined to succeed in forming a decisive judgment must devote considerable time to the matter. But then we may ask ourselves: Is it worth it? Our time is limited, and we have more profitable things to do.

[100]G. Rabeau, "Paroles surnaturelles et hallucinations auditives," "Comment discerner les paroles divines," "Le contenu des phénomènes mystiques," *Vie Spirituelle*, Supplement (November–December 1932 and February 1933).
[101]J. Lhermitte, "Origine et mécanisme des hallucinations," 128–129.

Even supposing that the revelation is really of divine origin, it is not too easy to be sure that the subject has understood it correctly. St. John has pointed out at length how inclined we are to take divine words in too material a sense. "Let us take an example," he says.

> A soul has great desires to be a martyr. It may happen that God answers him saying: "Thou shalt be a martyr." This will give him inwardly great comfort and confidence that he is to be martyred. Yet, notwithstanding, it may come to pass that he does not die the death of a martyr, and neverthe-less, the promise may be true.... Because it will be fulfilled according to the essential sense of that saying, namely, in that God will have given that soul the love and the reward which belong essentially to a martyr, and thereby making him a martyr of love.[102]

Hence, we cannot always pin our faith to the "letter" of a divine communication. And who does not know that sometimes sentences are uttered in an absolute form, the truth of which depends on some condition? The prophet Jonah knew that very well: just precisely for that reason, he refused to announce to the people of Nineveh that their city would be destroyed, when in the mind of God such a prophecy was perhaps only a threat; and he foresaw the possibility that the people would have remembered the foretelling, and would afterward mock him when they did not see his words fulfilled. So also the soul that hears a divine locution cannot be sure that it understands it aright.[103]

We must conclude that St. John is evidently perfectly aware of the difficulties raised by the problem of the "truth" of visions. He

---

[102] *Ascent*, bk. 2, chap. 19.
[103] *Ascent*, bk. 2, chap. 20.

even sees in these same difficulties and uncertainties a fundamental reason for not founding our spiritual life upon them. It would be absurd to build upon an unreliable foundation when a perfectly solid one exists. In the theological virtues, we possess this solid foundation, whereas visions are full of danger. Therefore, the saint instructs us to maintain a negative attitude toward the latter, but we must now consider carefully in what this consists in practice.

The Attitude Is Not Entirely Negative

I may say at once that there is no question of an entirely negative attitude. We shall see indeed that such enters, as an element, into a doctrine that is extremely positive. As we have already been reminded, St. John of the Cross inserts his teaching with regard to the use of visions in his more general exposition of the rules of conduct, whereby the soul is led to divine union by the short-est way. Knowing that the theological virtues are the proximate means of this union, he teaches the soul to nourish itself on these throughout all the circumstances of its life.

To proceed more clearly, we shall distinguish, with the saint, between what the soul should do at the actual moment when it receives the vision from what it should do afterward. Hence, we shall explain the more general question of the desire of visions and finish by examining some particular cases that seem to constitute an exception to the principles taught us by him. Our explanation will be both clarified and facilitated by the previous study of what we may call the "spiritual structure" of a supernatural vision.

The "Structure" of Visions

As we have seen, St. John of the Cross admits that, at times, God makes use of visions and interior words in order to help a soul to make progress in the spiritual life. But, seeing that all spiritual progress is fundamentally the work of divine grace, he teaches that every manifestation of a cognoscitive order made to a soul (it matters little whether it be a vision or a locution) is always accompanied by an interior grace that urges the soul to draw nearer to God. For the saint, the cognoscitive element offered to the understanding and the interior grace that impels the soul toward union with God are so intimately conjoined as to be comparable to the pulp and the rind of a fruit. The rind is the exterior—that is, the cognoscitive element of the vision—and the pulp of the fruit is the grace that interiorly inclines the soul toward God. Consequently, at the same moment that the soul "sees" the vision, it receives a grace that theology calls *gratia operante*—a grace that operates then and there. It is a precious grace, much more precious than the cognoscitive phenomenon that accompanies it, and the soul should try to profit by it in the best way.

When, in her youth, St. Teresa saw the apparition of Christ that reproached her for her dissipation, at the same moment she received a grace of compunction. If, instead of reflecting on the nature of her vision, she had profited by it to ask forgiveness for the sin she was committing, she might perhaps have been converted. Instead, she began to ponder over the possibility of such a vision and lost all the spiritual fruit of it. John of the Cross teaches the soul to benefit from the "pulp" of the fruit without wasting its energy uselessly in thinking about the "rind."[104]

Since the grace that comes to the soul is a grace *operante*, it does not depend on the soul's cooperation. The soul is, as it were, aroused by the apparition, but in order to receive the grace by which the said apparition is accompanied, it does not matter at all whether it considers the vision or attends to it or whether it

[104] *Ascent*, bk. 2, chaps. 11 and 17; bk. 3, chap. 13.

dismisses it from its mind. To be preoccupied with it is to risk losing the grace. In order that the grace may fructify in the soul, the latter must make use of it as soon as it receives it. For instance, if a soul sees Christ, the grace urges it to love Him; if it desires to profit thereby, forthwith it sets itself to love. For this, it will make an act of faith in His Godhead and follow it up by an intense act of charity. So the soul immediately practices the theological virtues. If, instead of this, it loses its time speculating about the vision in order to take pleasure in it or to feed its curiosity, far from being recollected, it is distracted and therefore will not profit by the grace offered to it. It has preferred the "rind" to the fruit.

In prescribing this attitude to the soul, St. John is merely applying his general principle: in order to attain to union with God, nothing is to be preferred to the practice of the theological virtues! Consequently, if confronted with a vision, the soul cannot do better than recollect itself in order to profit by the interior grace that is offered to it. So doing, it neglects the rind in order to feed upon the substance of the fruit. If need arise, it will consider the former later on.

Refer Everything to the Confessor

It will consider the former later on? And why?

First and foremost, in order to refer the matter to the confessor or spiritual director.

For the Mystical Doctor, this point of teaching is fundamental: the soul cannot direct itself in the ways of the spiritual life—not only because "no man can be a judge in his own case," but especially because we must work out our sanctification in the body of the Church and under her control.

This spiritual society, called "the Church," was founded by Our Lord to procure our sanctification. Therefore, to her has been entrusted the governance of souls, which she carries out by the ecclesiastical laws *in foro externo* and by spiritual direction *in foro interno*. In a matter so delicate and abstruse as that of apparitions, more than ever will this sound doctrine find its application.

St. John's teaching is clear: "Anything, of whatsoever kind, received by the soul through supernatural means, must at once be communicated to the spiritual director, clearly and plainly, entirely and simply."[105] But this is supposing that the confessor, or person consulted, possesses the necessary knowledge. Should it happen that the subject cannot find such a one in his environment, he will do better to say nothing and wait for a more favorable opportunity. Yet, be it noted, in this case, he is obliged not to attach any importance to the vision. The principle is categorical: "If such an expert person cannot be found, it is better to attach no importance to such words and to repeat them to nobody."[106]

Acting thus, the subject is freed from much preoccupation. He is not responsible for deciding whether his vision be true or not; it is enough that he refer all to his director; the latter will judge of the matter and, should there be anything to be done, will tell him. In the meantime, the subject knows what to do when anything of the kind occurs: throw away the "rind" and feed on the fruit; recollect himself in an act of loving faith, seek God in his inmost heart, and so profit by the invitation received by means of the vision.

"But," someone will say, "if I must refer it all to my director, I must pay close attention to it. Otherwise, I shall forget everything."

"Let it alone! If you forget it, that is a sign that it is not worth your while to attend to it."

[105] *Ascent*, bk. 2, chap. 22.
[106] *Ascent*, bk. 2, chap. 30.

Visions that are really supernatural remain imprinted upon the memory and even in the depths of the soul.[107] To force oneself to attend to them and remember them is to run great risk of mingling one's own activity therewith and opening the door to illusion.

"And if the divine words enjoin something upon me, ought I not to obey at once? It is God who is speaking!"

On no account whatever! The soul cannot move a step in this matter without a director's advice.[108] This rule admits of no exception. Even though he were perfectly certain of the divine origin of the locution, the subject must abide by the decision of his spiritual father. When speaking of those very rare cases in which, seemingly, the fullness of the spirit of prophecy is in action, and makes the revealed truth to be clearly known, St. John declares: "Yet although the soul holds something which it understands to be quite certain and true, and although it may be unable to give that passive interior consent, it must not therefore cease to believe and to give the consent of reason to that which its spiritual director tells it and commands it, even though this may be quite contrary to its own feelings."[109] It is still the application of the principle that proclaims the primacy of the Church's authority over all private inspirations. And it is necessary to insist upon this: we sanctify ourselves in the Church and under the guidance of her authority.

It was thus that St. Teresa always understood the matter, and when constrained by Fr. Gratian, her superior, to go on another foundation and not that which Our Lord had shown her, she obeyed with the utmost dispatch and simplicity. When subsequently asked

[107] *Life*, chap. 25; *Castle*, Sixth Mansion, chap. 3; *Ascent*, bk. 3, chap. 13.

[108] *Castle*, Sixth Mansion, chap. 3.

[109] *Ascent*, bk. 2, chap. 26.

by Gratian himself why she had not objected, seeing that she knew very well, on the testimony of learned priests, that she was guided by the Holy Spirit, she replied: "Because faith tells me that the orders of Your Reverence are the expression of the will of God, whereas I am never sure of *my* revelations." There spoke the true daughter of the Church! Such is the answer of a soul exquisitely Catholic!

Again, it may happen that the matter of a revelation is delicate. There may be times when its object is to reveal the sins of another. Woe to the imprudent visionary if he assumes that he has a mission to correct the party concerned! It will not always be a case of carrying out the brotherly admonition taught by Our Lord in the Gospel! Calumnies, quarrels, and unkindness are the sad results of his tempestuous intervention. Hence, it is not superfluous to consult someone whose judgment is mature.

On the other hand, a little more freedom of action may be allowed when the locution is nothing more than an admonition for the one who is receiving it. It would be ridiculous if someone who heard a voice saying, "Be humble!" were to put off making an act of humility until he could consult his confessor! Practice the virtuous act, not because you hear the voice but because you see that it is the right thing to do. The locution is here quite accidental; it should not be the motive for the decision, but it may accompany the latter without danger.[110]

The Memory of the Visions

The rule of complete detachment with respect to visions, which St. John imposes, does not apply only to the moment in which they are received; he lays down also that they are not to be stored up in the memory but are to be forgotten as soon as possible.

---

[110] *Castle*, Sixth Mansion, chap. 3.

Anyone who reads the works of St. Teresa and notices the esteem that that saint openly shows for the favors granted to her will be left somewhat astonished at this attitude. On this point, is there perhaps some disagreement between the two saints of the Carmel?

I do not think so. St. John's fundamental reason for forbidding the recipient to forget these favors is the general one already explained: visions are not immediate means of union with God; the practice of the theological virtues is much more efficacious. It is far more profitable to nourish oneself upon faith and charity than to cherish the memory of visions and revelations. Withal, St. John asserts that there are cases in which such favors are endowed with a peculiar property. Deeply impressed as they are upon the memory or even in the depths of the soul, the memory of them arouses a loving recollection. The valuable spiritual fruit produced by such graces may be a reason for recalling them from time to time.[111]

When St. Teresa shows esteem for her visions, she is wont to give as her reason the evident spiritual improvement that they cause in the soul. She feels more deeply recollected in her mental prayer when she remembers the gentle countenance of that *Only Good* of whom she had caught a passing glimpse one day. "The soul derives great profit from this favour ... for thinking upon Him, or upon His life and Passion, recalls His most meek and lovely face, which is the greatest consolation.... I assure you that such a delectable remembrance gives the greatest help and comfort."[112] Hence, her attitude does not seem irreconcilable with that of the Mystical Doctor. The memory of the vision carries her on to God.

Yet St. John insists: it is not the memory, as such, that must be esteemed but the good effect derived from it by the soul for its life

---

[111] *Ascent*, bk. 3, chaps. 13 and 14.
[112] *Castle*, Sixth Mansion, chap. 9.

of recollection. Consequently, no sooner has the soul been thus aided in its prayer by opportunely recalling some supernatural manifestation than it should be careful to withdraw its attention forthwith, in order to occupy itself wholly in the act of recollection whereby it enters into contact with God.[113] And so, once more, we are back at our theological virtues.

It is clear from this that even in the mortification of the memory, the saint's teaching does not run into extremes. He knows how to distinguish between different cases. But it is not rare to come across souls that distract their attention by scrutinizing the vision and complacently cherish the memory of certain such favors, seeing in them a sign of their sanctity. Folly and waste of time! How much better would it be to spend the time in practicing the virtues!

Visions Are Not to Be Desired

On one point, however, the doctrine of the Mystical Doctor is indeed absolute: visions are not to be desired. This is a prohibition that allows of no exception. In this attitude, St. Teresa had already preceded him. She mentions it when speaking of imaginary visions, but the motives upon which she bases her teaching apply to all kinds without distinction. Speaking of the exciting of our fancy that results from such a desire, she writes in the *Castle*: "With such a desire, a person is quite certain to be deceived or to be in great peril of being so.... When a person has a great desire for something, he persuades himself that he is seeing or hearing what he desires, just as those who go about desiring something all day dream of it at night."[114]

---

[113] *Ascent*, bk. 3, chap. 13.
[114] *Castle*, Sixth Mansion, chap. 9.

Another motive, and also one that holds good under all circumstances, is that to cherish such a desire is to depart from that *abandonment* to the divine will wherein consists our perfection. God knows better than we what way suits us best; to want to choose for ourselves would be absurd, especially when it is a question of choosing an extraordinary way.[115]

St. John has gone more deeply into the matter. In particular, he has examined the case of persons who dare to ask God to give them an answer by supernatural means. Having had some revelation that they believe has come from on high, they consider themselves justified in so acting, and they think that God should remove their theoretical and practical doubts. It even happens that the directors or admirers of such people wish by their means to obtain direction from God as to their own lives. The visionary is considered as a sort of oracle to be consulted and who can transmit the answer from Heaven.

Happenings such as these do not belong to the past of the Middle Ages! I happened to come across the case of an intelligent person — albeit in this matter, she scarcely showed herself to be such — who wished to question the Lord by means of a visionary in order to learn the future and know how to behave in a very difficult circumstance of her life. Only on my formal prohibition did she desist. Otherwise, who knows into what compromising position she might have brought herself? I have known a religious superior who thus inquired of God concerning the government of his community — and discovered later that the whole affair was fraudulent!

The proceeding is highly dangerous, declares St. John; and not only that: it is unlawful. It is highly dangerous because it opens the door to the intervention of the evil one.

[115] *Castle,* Sixth Mansion, chap. 9.

When anyone thus inquires of God, "sometimes the answer comes from the devil."[116] We know that he can exercise a certain influence upon our sensitive powers and cause in them phenomena similar to those of supernatural visions. He cannot do so unless God so permits, but

> in proportion as God is guiding the soul and communing with it, He gives the devil leave to act with it after this manner;[117] insinuating himself, like the wolf in sheep's clothing among the flock, with a success so nearly complete that he can hardly be recognized. For since he says many things that are true and in conformity with reason, and things that come to pass as he describes them, it is very easy for the soul to be deceived and to think that since these things happen as he says, and the future is correctly fore-told, this can be the work of none save God.... And since the devil has a very clear light of this kind, he can very eas-ily deduce effect from cause [and so predict the future].[118]

According to the saint, this power of the evil spirit reaches very far. He can foretell pestilences, earthquakes, divine punishments, death, all with at least a high degree of probability. From the fact that sometimes the predictions are exactly fulfilled, however, we must not hold that their divine origin is thereby proved. Often such are nothing but diabolical divination.

The reasons wherewith St. John shows that such inquiries are also unlawful are very similar to those that forbid us to consult fortune-tellers. "It is lawful to no creature to pass beyond the limits that God

---

[116] *Ascent*, bk. 2, chap. 21.
[117] *Dark Night*, bk. 2, chap. 23.
[118] *Ascent*, bk. 2, chap. 21.

has ordained for His governance, according to the laws of nature. In His governance of man, He has laid down rational and natural limits; wherefore, to desire to pass beyond them is not lawful, and to desire to seek out and attain to anything by supernatural means is to go beyond these natural limits."[119] He concludes: "I cannot see how the soul that desires these things can fail to commit at least venial sin, however good may be its aims and however far advanced it may be on the road to perfection; and he that bids the soul desire them, and consents to it, sins likewise."[120] The saint brings strong reasons to support his solid instruction: "There is no necessity for any of these things, since there is natural reason and an evangelical doctrine and law which are quite sufficient for the soul's guidance, and there is no difficulty or necessity that cannot be solved and remedied by these means."[121] Nay more, not to be contented with these, and to wish to inquire of God further, after the revelation made to us by Jesus Christ, seems to the saint an insult to God. "In giving us His divine Son, as He has done, who is His Word, and He has no other, God has spoken to us all together, once and for all in this single Word; and He has no occasion to speak further.... Wherefore, he that would now inquire of God, or seek any vision or revelation, would not only be acting foolishly, but would be committing an offense against God by not setting his eyes altogether upon Christ, and seeking no new thing or aught beside."[122]

How true this is! We have but one Master, even in the highest ways of the spiritual life. *Magister vester unus est, Christus:*[123] Christ

---

[119] *Ascent*, bk. 2, chap. 21.
[120] *Ascent*, bk. 2, chap. 21.
[121] *Ascent*, bk. 2, chap. 21.
[122] *Ascent*, bk. 2, chap. 22.
[123] "One is your master, Christ" (Matt. 23:10).

Jesus, who taught us during His life, and now perpetuates His teaching in Holy Church. To seek another is to withdraw from the divine plan of our spiritual restoration: *Instaurare omnia in Christo.*[124]

Manifestations of the Divine Attributes

And yet is not that true which Our Lord taught us: "He that loveth me shall be loved of my Father, and I will love him, and will manifest myself to him [*manifestabo ei meipsum*]" (John 14:21)?

Yes, there are manifestations of God that are the crown of a life of love. St. John knew them, but he distinguishes these completely from private visions and revelations. The latter have a distinct object; they are forms and figures; they are truths that present the form of distinct concepts; they are things that, although supernatural, bear the human imprint, the imprint of this limited and created world. But the mystical life knows of other manifestations that have not this limited and restricted form. St. John mentions certain "divine touches" that give to the soul an inexpressible sense of the divine perfections. They are graces wherein the soul, while rejoicing in the intimate presence of God in the depths of its substance, enjoys also in its intelligence "a substantial perception of some divine attribute."[125] When He communicates Himself to the soul, God can make it experience His power, dominating it irresistibly, unto the last "roots" of its being and its working; or He can even insinuate Himself so gently into its center as to fill it superabundantly with His infinite sweetness. St. Teresa also speaks of certain graces in which God makes the soul, as it were, "recognize" Him.[126] These are very high graces that suppose, however,

---

[124] "To restore all things in Christ." Motto of Pope St. Pius X.
[125] *Ascent*, bk. 2, chap. 26.
[126] *Castle*, Sixth Mansion, chap. 4.

that the soul has attained to mystical union, of which they are the connatural complement. "They are part of the union,"[127] writes the Mystical Doctor, in this connection. Here there is no longer anything that can hinder or retard that union; we are dealing with one of its consequences; with its crowning grace!

The saint counsels a very different attitude in regard to these graces; since there is no longer any question of distinct and particular communications of created things, he no longer reiterates: *No admitir!* The soul should receive these "unitive" graces with unspeakable gratitude, as it would receive from God's hand a vast treasure. Prudence may advise us not to cherish an explicit desire for such favors, in order not to expose ourselves to some illusion by confusing them with phenomena that are greatly inferior to them; but we are by no means to exclude them from the horizons of our contemplative ideal. It may even be said that in them consists the highest contemplation. We go out from the order of particular visions to enter into that of *union.* "The soul must be humble and resigned concerning them, and let God perform His work how and when He wills."[128] "God gives Himself wholly to the soul that gives itself wholly to Him."[129]

These graces call for an exceptional attitude because they are met with at the end of the road, because they are "part of the Union." But even when still on the way, we meet with certain favors that call for a similar attitude. They are the "substantial words which immediately fulfill in the soul what they signify."[130] The soul

---

[127] *Ascent,* bk. 2, chap. 26.

[128] *Ascent,* bk. 2, chap. 26.

[129] *Life,* chap. 27; *Conceptions of the Love of God,* chap. 5, no. 5; chap. 6, no. 9.

[130] *Ascent,* bk. 2, chap. 31.

hears the words "Love me," and at the same instant it feels itself very strongly moved to love God. In this case, as St. John observes, the soul has nothing to do; it is God who is working in it and, at the same time, showing it what He is doing. The words are a true, passive communication of supernatural life, and their value lies not in the words themselves, which, even in this case, are but "the rind," but in the passive efficacious grace that accompanies them. "Happy the soul to whom God speaks in such a manner."[131] The words heard by St. Teresa were often of this kind.

Notwithstanding, we must not think that St. John attaches a certain importance to the words heard by the soul or that he allows it to desire to hear such a locution. No, he remains faithful to his fundamental principles, and these never permit us to desire distinct divine communications but concentrate our desires upon union with God and the immediate means thereto. The passive communication of supernatural life, which accompanies the "substantial" word, undoubtedly includes an actuation of the theological virtues and consequently, directly promotes union with God; here we have the reason why it is to be highly esteemed. The "substantial" words are an outer skin that contains such a grace; if they are precious, it is because of the presence of this grace. But insofar as the actual "rind" is concerned, here also, if we are to be faithful to the saint, we must repeat: *No admitir!*

Conclusion

St. John of the Cross has treated the question of the soul's attitude in a manner marked by both solidity and delicate discrimination. The solidity of his teaching is derived from its firm foundations.

[131] *Ascent*, bk. 2, chap. 31.

Theology clearly demonstrates that it would be unreasonable to become attached to visions and to build our spiritual life upon them. They are not proximate means of union with God—that function being reserved to the theological virtues. Moreover, they expose the soul to many dangers of illusion that cannot easily be avoided.

Far from constituting a problem that the subject or his director must solve before anything can be done, the difficulty of judging as to the origin of the visions is the underlying reason for the attitude of reserve prescribed by the saint. On no account must we support our spiritual life upon such unsafe foundations, when we have at our disposal other means that will lead us safely to the goal we desire to reach: the theological virtues.

Consequently, all exaggerated esteem for visions must be banished. It is even preferable that we should prefer not to meet with such phenomena in our spiritual lives and should be loath to believe in their authenticity. No attitude is safer than this.

But even while it remains solidly founded upon general principles, St. John's doctrine remains full of discrimination. His *No admitir!* is not an absolute and untouchable law that means to treat of visions as though such things could never be. He allows that there may be true visions, even on the exterior or imaginary planes; he does not exclude the possibility that we may sometimes take account of such, but, in this case, we are always to follow the advice of another.

So there is no absolutism; there is not even crude negation. St. John teaches us how we should profit by the visions, though not in the manner that many people imagine. There is no question of analyzing the cognoscitive phenomena presented to the soul that often arouse its curiosity. Rather, must we forget this outer covering in order to savor the fruit of grace that is hidden therein and go forward in the holy recollection of loving faith that leads to union with God.

Consequently, we are not to reject everything in the visions! Indeed, the saint mentions two cases in which the so-called revelation resolves itself, or almost does so, into a grace of light and love. Indistinct revelations of the divine attributes, which the soul may receive in the highest unitive contemplation, are not devoid of anything that the soul may and ought to accept. They are graces of union, wherein the soul rejoices at the end of its spiritual journey. But these graces are no longer revelations in the commonly accepted sense of the word. Ordinarily speaking, by "revelations" and "visions" we understand divine communications that have a determined character, that are distinct, conceptual—in short, human; these others, on the contrary, are not determined, not conceptual, but superhuman. Besides these, there are "substantial words" that immediately bring about in the soul what they announce and that constitute another exception. Yet, this is not because they are *words*, but because they are *substantial*—that is, because they passively convey an efficacious grace. Here also, it is not the outer covering but the fruit that is of value.

Withal, it is not to be denied that the "rind" also may be worth something; therefore, the saint would have the subject relate everything to his confessor. The latter will decide the matter. St. John has freed the soul from the harassing problem of discerning as to its revelations. He has not seen fit to supply it with the criteria whereby it can judge whether a vision comes from God; he has not thought it worthwhile.[132] Whatever be the source of a phenomenon, the soul receiving it can never do better than recollect itself. If it happens that some command is enjoined by this means, the subject will refer it to his director, and the latter will consider it.

[132] *Ascent*, bk. 2, chap. 18.

Notwithstanding this, by thus referring the penitent to his confessor, the saint has not suppressed but has only transferred one of the most difficult problems raised by the visions. Ought we now to hearken to what is told us by these means? Does it not seem that such a problem forces us back to that other problem, so difficult of solution, of the origin of visions? For it is true that only in the case of their coming from God can there be any question of carrying out what is commanded under such circumstances.

The saint's teaching has demonstrated that the attitude enjoined upon the soul from the outset is based not directly upon the examination of the visions but upon the fundamental principles of the spiritual life and upon the general conditions of these phenomena; but the solution of a special problem that we cannot ignore now seems to raise once more, and in all its urgency, the very question we had hoped to avoid.

On this account, we should have no hesitation in declaring that St. John's teaching was incomplete if, after having referred the difficulty to the confessor, he had not instructed the latter how to act in order to satisfy the legitimate inquiries of the penitent. But he had not shrunk from this difficult task. In the following chapter, we shall see how, on this subject also, his doctrine is really complete and fulfills all the requirements of spiritual direction.

So far, he has shown himself the safest of guides in the way of union with God. With enlightened prudence, he secures the soul from all danger of straying, all occasions of illusion. Not only so, but amid the dangers, he urges it on in the way that leads most directly to union by the practice of the theological virtues. We need not feel at all humiliated in going to the school of such a teacher. He repays our docility richly and *gives us security in the most important undertaking of our whole life: the achievement of union between our soul and God.*

4

The Attitude of the Director

St. John of the Cross has greatly simplified the problem of visions for the soul that receives them. The latter is to find in them solely an occasion for recollecting itself more deeply in God; for the rest, it will simply refer the whole matter to its director and abide by his opinion. Even when there is question of carrying out some command believed to be divine, without his approval the subject must not move a step.

However, this very freeing of the subject from responsibility involves a greater responsibility for the director, since every decision as to the value of the communications received devolves in practice upon him. In particular, he will have to decide whether it is well to give any credit to the invitations or orders received by this channel. But how can he do this until he has made up his mind whether the communication comes from God or not? Is it not just because it believes that such is the case that the soul wishes to follow out such instructions? This time it does seem as though the director will be forced to face the problem of the nature and origin of the visions. By lightening the burden of the penitent, the saint has merely increased that of the director. Now at least, the latter may well believe that only specialists are capable of guiding souls favored with visions.

I think not!

Visions and Revelations

The object of this chapter is to show how, taking his stand upon the instructions of St. John of the Cross, a director may give excellent advice to souls, even as regards obeying an order received by revelation, without being compelled to go into all the difficulties involved by the discernment of visions. Not, indeed, that he should be entirely uninterested in the latter question. Many reasons may render it advisable that he should seek at least an approximate solution. Consequently, we shall determine how far the discerning of visions is of importance for spiritual direction and try to show what is the best method.

Ground the Soul in Faith

A synthetic writer can fit particular problems perfectly into the framework of his doctrine. Set thus immediately in the light of the principles that govern a whole science, they at once derive therefrom the beginning of a solution; the adequate solution needed will even, for the most part, result from a more precise application of these principles to the fresh data from which the problem has arisen. St. John of the Cross is an eminently synthetic thinker, and he has envisaged the problem of visions and revelations in the light of the more fundamental principles of the spiritual life.

Seeing that the purpose of his teaching is to obtain the closest union with God possible on Earth, and to point out the shortest and safest way thereto, he emphasizes the primary importance of the theological virtues in attaining this sublime end. They, and they alone, are the immediate means leading to that union. The soul's whole spiritual interest lies in grounding its life more securely upon these virtues or, to use the saint's characteristic expression, in following "the way of faith." Correlatively, the director's fundamental duty is to "root and ground" the soul in faith, seeing that it belongs to him to help it along the road of perfection.

As a good shepherd, the director, in all his relations with souls, must always lead his sheep to the most nourishing pastures and keep them away not only from what is definitely bad for them but from all that may be merely doubtfully safe. He must not risk their precious lives, especially when healthy and safe food is to be found in abundance.

This means that there are two sides to the attitude that characterizes a good director. Since he is a lover of what is safe and solid, he cultivates in souls a love for the theological virtues, and on the other hand, he does his best to keep them from all hankering after what is extraordinary and even from all exaggerated esteem for these graces, which, although of value when authentic, remain open to many deceptions.

Nevertheless, not all priests are thus prudent, and in this connection, St. John remarks: "In certain spiritual masters, I have observed a lack of discretion."[133] Even in our day, some directors attach too much importance to visions, are too fond of them, and are too inclined to welcome them confidently. St. John considers this disposition most dangerous. "Trusting to these supernatural apprehensions ... both masters and disciples have fallen into great error and found themselves in sore straits. Wherein is fulfilled the saying of Our Lord: *If the blind lead the blind, both fall into the ditch.* He does not say that they will fall, but that they fall; since the very venturing of the one to guide the other is a going astray."[134]

A case came to my knowledge of a young woman, who seemed indeed really virtuous, who confided to her director that an interior voice was speaking to her. Forthwith, he accepted it as wholly divine. One day, this voice informed the person in question that

[133] *Ascent,* bk. 2, chap. 18.
[134] *Ascent,* bk. 2, chap. 18.

after her death, which would occur before long, her life must be published. In order not to lose time, her director made her write her autobiography at once. I have had it in my hands; only the final chapter, relating to her death, was wanting, because ... the young woman had not died at the time foretold! The least that can be said is that there was no necessity for such great haste, and no need for anyone to let himself be drawn into such puerile nonsense!

So convinced is St. John that the greatest discretion is necessary for the spiritual guide when dealing with visions that he has no hesitation in advising subjects to leave a director whom they perceive lacks this quality. "When the spiritual father has this inclination toward visions," says the saint, "and takes pleasure in them, it is impossible but that he will impress that delight, and that desire upon the spirit of his disciple, even without realizing it."[135]

It is only to be expected that the latter will be influenced by the former, since "the spirit of the disciple grows in conformity with that of his master, in a hidden and secret way."[136] Rather than expose oneself to that subtle contagion, it is better to withdraw in time.

The saint condemns categorically in the director any course of action that may generate in his penitent a particular esteem for visions. It is a mistake to speak too much of the matter to the latter, in such wise "as to devote the greater part of his spiritual conversation to them."[137] How do you expect him not to esteem what you are continually talking about? For this reason, it does not benefit the director to discuss with his penitent the signs whereby true visions may be distinguished from false ones. "Although it

---

[135] *Ascent*, bk. 2, chap. 18.
[136] *Ascent*, bk. 2, chap. 18.
[137] *Ascent*, bk. 2, chap. 18.

is well to know this, there is no reason for causing the soul this labour, anxiety, and peril."[138] It becomes the disciple to obey and to abide by the confessor's decision.

For all that, it seems only too true that, in certain cases, exactly the contrary takes place; St. John knows of some directors "who, when they see that their penitents are receiving visions from God, beg them to entreat Him to reveal such and such things to them … and the foolish souls do so, thinking that it is lawful to desire knowledge by this means."[139] With such, the Mystical Doctor is very severe and has stated expressly that such a proceeding is not without sin.[140]

If he is to ground souls in faith, the director has much to avoid, but that is not enough. Besides the negative, there must be also the positive attitude, in which we must yet distinguish different stages according to the diversity of the facts presented. The case of a passing phenomenon is one thing; that of persistent and repeated communications is quite another; locutions that order the subject to do something present yet a different case. In the last event, a fresh question arises: Must such orders be obeyed?

The Duty of Listening to the Subject

Although it is true that a director ought not to show himself highly interested as soon as a spiritual child makes any mention of a vision, neither, on the other hand, ought he to close the slide of the confessional grille nervously, in order to dismiss the importunate penitent who is making him waste precious time with his or her nonsense! If he is certain that it really is nonsense, he may even

[138] *Ascent*, bk. 2, chap. 18.
[139] *Ascent*, bk. 2, chap. 18.
[140] *Ascent*, bk. 2, chap. 21.

act thus; but if he has to do with a sensible person, he should not pass judgment a priori, seeing that, as St. John of the Cross teaches, sometimes God does really make use of such means in order to promote a soul's spiritual welfare.[141] Moreover, we must be logical. If the penitent has the duty of referring everything to the director, the director likewise has the duty of listening to the penitent. Again, St. John never allows that it is right to treat souls roughly; rather, they should be treated with the authority belonging to a father and a teacher. The saint wants directors to know also how to use this authority in order to make it easier for souls to speak of these favors received from God. Not all such people are chatterboxes who take an obvious pleasure in talking about themselves and whom it is well to cut short. There do exist humble folk who are very timid in relating such matters "because they see not why they should have these experiences, which seem to belong to saints."[142] With these, the Mystical Doctor wishes the confessors "to proceed very quietly and kindly, encouraging these souls, and giving them an opportunity to speak of these things. If necessary, they should be exhorted to speak."[143]

Show Opposition at First

But there is no need to act thus from the first moment that a subject mentions some vision. Since there exist elements of such doubtful nature, the very discussion of which may be already a waste of time, it would be well at first for the director to seek simply to set them aside. And sometimes he will succeed in so doing. The fact is that there are people whose imagination is too vivid, who are disposed

---

[141] See the preceding chapter.
[142] *Ascent*, bk. 2, chap. 22.
[143] *Ascent*, bk. 2, chap. 22.

to take for visions the unreliable illusions of that faculty. "This is a great weakness, especially in women," writes St. Teresa, "so soon as anything disturbs our fancy, we must not forthwith think about visions. When there is question of true visions, believe me, they are very clearly known for such."[144]

Some simple souls can confuse certain tricks of their imagination with visions and even excite these still more just by attaching importance to them. On the other hand, sometimes it will be enough to ignore them in order to get rid of them. On this principle, nothing is more reasonable than to let the whole matter drop. "Pay no attention to this, my child. Do not busy yourself about it; it is enough to think of God." Moreover, there need not be the slightest fear lest this prudent attitude may do harm to God's working. St. Teresa of Jesus reassures us, "I believe that it is always better for them to resist such things at first; for if they are of God, resisting them will serve only to increase them since, being put to the proof, they will occur more and more."[145]

Teresa is speaking from her own experience. Remember that, in her case, her confessors were anything but encouraging! They strove, by every means in their power, to withdraw her from this perilous way, and to this end, they undertook a veritable crusade of prayers.

The Soul Should Be Recollected

Nothing is of any use, however, when God wills to lead a soul by this path. The persistent recurrence of the phenomena will show the director that it is impossible to ignore them. "I cannot help it, Father," confides the penitent to the priest, who has been advising

---

[144] *Foundations*, chap. 8.
[145] *Castle*, Sixth Mansion, chap. 3.

him to pay no attention to the locutions that he said he was hearing. "The words I hear are so clearly spoken that it is impossible not to hear them; so definite that I cannot help but understand their sense, and they always urge me to greater fervor." It would be useless to insist further, and St. Teresa warns us in this matter: "The soul should not be allowed to become distressed or disquieted, for it really cannot help itself."[146] Therefore, the director will grant that these phenomena really exist in the soul; he should bear this in mind when advising it, but even now, he must not forget his fundamental duty: *to settle the soul in faith.*

To tell the truth, he cannot as yet pronounce as to the origin of the phenomena, but whatever it be, he can maintain an attitude that will be profitable in any case: the subject should not occupy itself with the revelations but should profit by these in order to be more deeply recollected in God. It is never a bad thing to practice recollection; it is an excellent means of avoiding the illusions of the evil one, and in case the revelation be divine, nothing better can be done. The director will remember St. John's teaching with respect to the "spiritual structure" of visions: a vision is made up of a twofold element of unequal value. The intellectual communication is but the outer casing, enclosing a fruit of grace that urges the soul forward on the way of union with God. There is no better manner of cooperating with this grace than by recollecting oneself in an act of loving faith.

"Do not worry about this," the spiritual father will reply to the penitent who informs him of the repeated occurrence of his revelations, "for all of this is not of much importance; but every time you hear these interior words, without delaying to examine into the sense of them and even without attending to them, turn

---

[146] *Castle*, Sixth Mansion, chap. 3.

at once to God and try to be deeply recollected with Our Lord, who is dwelling in your heart. That is what He wants of you."

Perhaps then the penitent may hesitate and suggest some doubt: "Father, is it not failing in reverence for Our Lord not to take account of the words He says to me?"

"Be at peace. The words you hear speak of perfection, but what is far more important is God's invitation to you. He wants you to be wholly His, lovingly occupied with Him, who is present in the center of your soul. That must be your principal care."

Substantial Words

"Father," resumes the spiritual child, a few weeks later, "I have followed your advice and found it works very well. Every time Jesus comes, I feel gently moved to enter into myself, and often after such a grace, I remain for a long time in this quiet prayer, in which I do nothing but busy myself lovingly with Him. But during the last few days, something new has happened."

"What?"

"Father, it was one day when I was feeling very upset, even wretched, at the thought that I could not succeed in loving God as I want to love Him. Now, all at once, Jesus came to me and said these words: 'Love me!' My whole soul seemed changed, as by enchantment, and I felt seized upon by an immense, loving force that impressed itself upon my will and drew me to God."

"What did you do then?"

"I did as I always do: obeyed. I did not stop to consider where these words came from, and I set myself with all my heart to follow the divine attraction that was so strongly urging me to love. As a result, I seemed to receive a strong invitation to be very generous, and this proved useful some hours later when I had to face a great trouble and difficulty."

"You have done right. Go on as you are doing."

"But, Father, do these words really come from God?"

"Graces of this sort are among the safest, but it is much better for you not to analyze them. Be content to heed God's call to you to be recollected, even when such an invitation comes to you in a more powerful manner. You can never show your gratitude better than by keeping your heart free from every useless preoccupation in order to bend all your efforts to loving God intensely."

A Work to Carry Out

Some months go by, and the spiritual child reports to her director: "Father, it seems as though Our Lord wants something from me. He has made me see more clearly something that I had noticed myself some time ago. There are so many poor working girls in our parish who, owing to a lack of the good Christian training that would preserve them from moral dangers, are exposed to the peril of losing their innocence in the factories of the town. 'They are all mine,' Our Lord said to me, and I felt He wanted me to do something about it. What ought I to do?"

"I must think about it, child. Talk to me about it again later."

The fact is that a fresh problem is forcing itself upon the director. The communication made to the soul no longer concerns only its spiritual welfare. An activity is being enjoined that is concerned not with the spiritual profit of the subject but with that of others. Should he approve or not?

In order to decide, does it not seem as though now, at least, the director must make up his mind as regards the nature of the revelations?

Once again, St. John will help him out of this difficult position. Not even in this case need he pass a definitive judgment as to the quality of the communication the soul has received. There is another way that will lead to the end: that of reason based upon faith. "There is natural reason, and an evangelical doctrine and law which are quite sufficient for the soul's guidance, and there is no difficulty or necessity that cannot be solved and remedied by these means.... If certain things be told us supernaturally ... we must receive only that which is in clear conformity with reason and evangelical law; and then we must receive it not because it is revelation, but because it is reason."[147]

This solid doctrine of the Mystical Doctor clearly indicates to the director the line he should take. He should answer the practical difficulty laid before him by his penitent "according to reason enlightened by faith"; that is, he must decide in the light of the gospel principles whether the work suggested by the supernatural locution be opportune. The said locution is reduced to the role of a simple "stimulus" and should not even weigh in the balance. If he concludes that the work ought to be undertaken, it must be *because he sees that it is opportune*, not because it has been revealed.

And that was how St. Teresa used to act when beginning the work of her reform. Although God informed her that this must be undertaken, she submitted her plan to her superior without mentioning the revelation she had received, and hence, the latter judged and approved of it according to reason and faith.[148] The director will do likewise in this case. He will look into the state of the parish, and perhaps he will see that there is a crying need for the work suggested by his penitent. Consequently, he will endeavor to establish a new activity of Catholic Action in which she will be able to take her place, whether as president or as an ordinary member. Further, in choosing for her one or another position, he

---

[147] *Ascent*, bk. 2, chap. 21.
[148] *Life*, chap. 32.

will take account of her qualifications and decide *according to reason*. Even should it happen that she was mistaken, nothing will have been done that does not call for approval. All will be conformable to reason and faith.

☙

Here, seemingly, we have succeeded in freeing the spiritual director, at least to a great extent, from the troublesome task of deciding as to the nature of the visions. Even without pronouncing a final opinion as regards their origin and structure, he can make up his mind whether a subject ought to carry out commands thus received or simply dismiss them from his or her mind. Hence, it may be taken as demonstrated that the problem of their qualification is not at all an urgent one for him. If, on the other hand, circumstances show that it is advisable to examine thoroughly into some particular case, he may seek help from others.

Discernment of Visions

When all is said and done, it must be granted that there is an aspect of this question that obviously arouses the director's interest. Given the fact that his penitent experiences these phenomena, either the latter is deluded by the devil, or by his own fanciful imagination, or else God Himself is assisting him in his progress toward sanctity by these means. Consequently, for the peace of the director as much as for that of the penitent, it is well that, at least after some time has gone by, the spiritual father should be able to distinguish whether the hand of the Lord may be recognized in some manner in these occurrences. We shall try, therefore, to offer also a solution of the discernment of the visions, the more so since we are persuaded that our conclusions will serve to confirm the very prudent attitude of St. John of the Cross.

The criteria for this purpose of discernment, which are to be found scattered about in the works of the different mystical writers who have treated of the matter, are sufficiently numerous, but all may be classed under three principal heads: (1) the condition of the subject who is having the visions, (2) the objective content of the phenomena, and (3) the effects that the visions produce in the subject. Not all these tests serve to show directly the divine influence; some lead merely to a sort of *nihil obstat*: that is to say, they do not exclude the possibility that God is intervening. We shall call these *negative*, reserving the name of *positive* for those that point directly to the divine intervention.

The Condition of the Subject

The examination of the subject may be undertaken from a double point of view: psychical and moral.

Taking account of the person's physical condition, we are able, in most cases, to eliminate the hypothesis of hallucination. We know, indeed, that hallucinations do offer characteristics similar to those of exterior and imaginary visions. The victim of hallucinations also sees figures not seen by the bystanders and hears words the latter do not hear; and there is nothing to hinder those words and appearances from being of a religious character.

But the man subject to hallucinations is physically *deficient*, as we can often see from certain characteristics: he is hyperexcitable and impressionable to an exaggerated degree. Usually he is very distressed when suffering from the hallucination and remains in a state of exhaustion and depression that, far from favoring the development of his moral qualities, tends rather to hinder it. And take notice that certain excesses in corporal austerities can produce such nervous debility, all of which, when it is notable, can be perceived by an observant director. On the other hand, in milder cases, these features are more apt to be hidden. In the case of a perfectly balanced subject, however, both possibilities may be ruled out.

Apart from a disposition to hallucination, a subject may show a tendency to illusion. A slight want of judgment, joined to a vivid imagination, sometimes leads people to take for visions what is merely the passing play of the fancy. Those who have seen a crucifix on the wall move its eyes or have smelled a perfume filling a room at certain moments are often merely under an illusion. Obviously, if a director has recognized that his penitent is subject to hallucinations, or merely open to illusions, he will cast no further thought to visions!

Among the *moral qualities*, what matters most to the director is his penitent's sincerity. The reason is obvious. He can know the experiences of his disciple only from the latter's account of them. If the penitent tells him untruths or simply exaggerates, the very basis of his judgment is falsified. However, it is not always a question of formal deception, but some persons are endowed with such a wonderful gift of "construction," joined sometimes to a peculiar power of assimilation in their reading, that they might pass for so many St. Teresas if the director were not quick enough to perceive the slightly theatrical flavor that marks their accounts. Moreover, sincerity is shown not only in speech; very often it shows itself chiefly in the general conduct of a life. A soul may be so candid and so humble as to preclude all doubt as to its sincerity. Such was the case with St. Teresa, as her companions and those who studied her always recognized.

Is it necessary that the soul favored with visions should be already a saint? Certainly not! In fact, it is evident, both in general teaching on the subject and in St. John of the Cross, that visions are met with in the Illuminative Way — hence, before the soul has reached perfection. All the same, it must be recognized that the visions are more likely to be reliable when met with in company with sanctity. St. Teresa has explicitly stated this, and the same idea is expressed by Benedict XIV in his treatise on canonization, in which he says that in considering causes of beatification, no account is to be taken of visions as an argument in favor of the sanctity of the subject until the heroicity of his virtues has been demonstrated.[149]

However, all the tests applied in examining the subject are only negative. A perfectly balanced temperament and moral qualities do not suffice to prove that his visions are of divine origin; but they suffice to prove the possibility that, at least in practice, is excluded in cases of persons subject to hallucinations or wanting in sincerity. In order to go further, we must apply other criteria.

The Content of the Visions

Analysis of the content of a vision may sometimes lead our search to a satisfactory conclusion.

The most easily demonstrated case of this sort is that of a prophetic revelation. A locution that causes someone to know beforehand, and clearly, a future free happening *naturally impossible to foresee* must come from God. It is true that it is not always easy to decide with certainty whether the fact is really unpredictable, and St. John of the Cross has reminded us appositely how widely extended is the power of divination possessed by the evil one,[150] but that such cases do exist no one can deny. When St. John of the Cross foretells a week beforehand the day, and subsequently

---

[149] *Life, chap.* 21; Benedictus XIV, *De Servorum Dei Beatificatione*, bk. III, chap. 52, no. 2.
[150] *Ascent*, Bk. 2, chap. 21.

the hour of his death, it seems obvious that we are confronted with a fact that could not be known so exactly by natural means. Such predictions are miracles of the intellectual order and must be attributed to the intervention of the charisma called the light of prophecy, which God infuses only *permodum transeuntis* (through a transitory impression)[151] to the one who prophecies.

Speaking of the prophets of the Old Testament, St. Thomas remarks that, when imparted in its full perfection, this light rendered evident for the prophet both the certainty of the objective communication and the actual fact of the divine revelation.[152] It is difficult to be sure that the prophetic lights communicated to souls in our day are always equally perfect. Yet St. John of the Cross, who had experience of this grace, remarks thereon that "when the soul is taught these truths, they sink into it deeply ... to such an extent that, although others may tell it something else, the soul cannot give its inward assent to them, even though it endeavour to give such assent by making a great effort, because ... it knows something else by means of the Spirit which teaches it that thing, which is equivalent to seeing it clearly."[153] Seemingly therefore, there is at least objective evidence; as to the subjective evidence, on the other hand—that is, on the evidence of the fact of the divine revelation—we find nothing explicit in the Doctor's works.

A far more delicate phenomenon than that of prophecy is the knowledge of the secrets of the human heart, although often this has been put on the same plane. It is clear that this also may be the effect of a divine enlightening, but often it will not be easy to ascertain. An admonition of St. John in this connection is only

---

[151] *Summa Theologica*, II-II, q. 171, art. 2.
[152] *Summa Theologica*, II-II, q. 171, art. 5.
[153] *Ascent*, bk. 2, chap. 26.

too well known. Even though reminding us that such knowledge may be due to a charismatic light, he adds: "Those whose spirits are purified can know *by natural means*, and some more readily than others, that which is in the inward spirit or heart of another … and this by outward indications, albeit very slight ones, as words, movements and other signs."[154] Therefore, the saint allows that there may be a kind of "introspection of the conscience of another" that he considers quite natural; it is not direct, however, but by means of outward signs, seemingly recognizable only by a "purified spirit." This teaching shows us how delicate a matter it is to pass judgment regarding the charismatic character of the gift that some saints possessed of reading the consciences of others. It was not prudent for a soul in mortal sin to come near St. Philip Neri; he soon made it blush! Yet it was a happy imprudence usually followed by the penitent sinner's receiving absolution from the same saint. How did St. Philip read the consciences of others? Immediately, by a charismatic light, or by means of the slight indications that his pure eye could perceive in the sinner's bearing? It seems difficult to give a general answer. Perhaps there was something of both. Obviously, however, this natural scrutiny is more restricted and less secure than that which is charismatic. We can understand, therefore, why St. John of the Cross requires a soul to be very cautious in making use of such a gift of perception in its relations with others.[155]

If it be so difficult to pronounce in individual cases upon these high phenomena characteristic of supernatural communications, no one will be surprised when we state that, in the majority of cases, the fact that a vision is believed to be of an "intellectual"

---

[154] *Ascent*, bk. 2, chap. 26.
[155] *Ascent*, bk. 2, chap. 26.

character is not enough to make us pronounce it divine. Besides the fact that not very many people are capable of recognizing such a character, we must notice that, even four times over,[156] St. John states that *by suggestion* the evil one can represent to the mind many items of intellectual knowledge. I believe that, in these cases, the imagination will always intervene in some way, but I repeat that, without good philosophical training, it is difficult for a person to be sure that the imagination has counted for nothing in the communication received. A vision of the mystery of the Blessed Trinity that seems rather an intuition, as was experienced by St. Teresa in the last ten years of her life, seems, necessarily, to require the intervention of a charismatic light; but the saint observed that sometimes there was added to it an imaginary representation that helped her to understand the mystery of the indwelling of the Trinity in our souls.[157] She derived therefrom a certain facility in speaking of so high a mystery. This shows us, however, that it is not enough for a soul to believe it enjoys a vision of the Trinity to be able to declare that such a vision is purely intellectual.

These considerations lead us to conclude that, in the vast majority of cases, we should in practice treat the phenomenon as though it were of the imaginary order. Yet once we come down to this plane, the analysis of the content can be only a negative test. Thus, if a locution were contradictory to the Faith (the ancient writers usually said contradictory to Holy Scripture) or to the truths naturally ascertained, we must exclude a divine origin; but in order to establish the latter, its accord with the truth would not be enough. Visions that are indecent, of a burlesque character, or

---

[156] *Ascent*, bk. 2, chaps. 24, 26, 29, and 31.
[157] *Spiritual Relations*, no. 22.

merely puerile cannot be considered divine. But even though they bear all the marks of gravity and nobility, that does not suffice to enable us to say that they come from God.

Thus, we must conclude that the first two classes of tests—those that we find in the subject and those that result from analyzing the content of the visions—are frequently only *negative*. To decide positively as to the divine intervention, we must turn to the third test: the data derived from the effects produced in the soul by the visions.

Effects of the Visions

As regards the use of these last tests, I would like to observe that not all mystical writers stress the strength of the argument based upon these, whereas others, on the contrary, think we may draw conclusions therefrom that the tests do not justify.

Speaking of these effects produced in the soul, many theologians are content to single out the feelings of peace, security, and moral strength that the visions cause after a first movement of amazement and fear, in contrast to diabolical visions, which at first produce a sense of joy, only to leave the soul subsequently troubled. I ask myself whether these feelings, considered so generally, can really serve as definitive proofs. The fact does not seem ruled out that natural phenomena of a religious aspect may, at least in some measure, produce similar feelings in a generally well-disposed soul.

On the other hand, even while confining himself to the spiritual effects, St. John of the Cross has spoken of them in a far more characteristic and clearly determined manner. He has shown plainly how these effects, which vary greatly as regards intensity and clearness, can also go so far as to constitute an evident reawakening of the supernatural life communicated to the soul in a manner that is clearly passive.

Then the visions are linked up with progress in the mystical life, the experimental character of which enables one to distinguish it more easily.

In connection with certain interior words, which St. John calls "formal," addressed to the soul "as by a third person," he plainly states that the effect that they produce is not great;[158] but he concludes precisely from this that, in this case, the test is insufficient.[159] Yet in other cases, "the effect is that of quiet, illumination, joy like that of glory, sweetness, purity, love; humility and inclination, or elevation of the spirit in God."[160] "The will is affectioned to God and inclined to well-doing."[161] Here the soul is already aware that under the impulse of these visions, it produces intense acts of spiritual life. This character of manifest spiritual benefit is more marked still in the case of certain visions that are imprinted in the depths of the soul; it suffices to recall them to feel drawn to God.[162] But the case in which, seemingly, they reach their peak point is that of the "substantial words" that "are of such moment and price that they are life and virtue and incomparable blessing to the soul.... Sometimes one of these words works a greater blessing in the soul than all that the soul has itself done throughout its life."[163] In this case, seeing itself obviously enriched with a great spiritual treasure, and that passively, the soul can have no doubt as to the author of this benefit. It can be only God. And therefore, when he treats of substantial words, although so

[158] *Ascent*, bk. 2, chap. 30.
[159] *Ascent*, bk. 2, chap. 30.
[160] *Ascent*, bk. 2, chap. 24.
[161] *Ascent*, bk. 2, chap. 29.
[162] *Ascent*, bk. 3, chap. 13.
[163] *Ascent*, bk. 2, chap. 31.

loath to admit of visions, St. John exclaims: "Happy the soul to whom God thus speaks!"[164]

St. Teresa also regarded this test of good dispositions, manifestly infused into the soul, as the surest sign of the divine origin of the phenomenon. "The first and truest sign is the sense of power and authority which they carry with them, both in themselves and in the actions that follow them."[165]

Evidently in cases in which the subject feels that he is mystically filled with love, or raised to divine contemplation, he can recognize the hand of God far more clearly than when it is solely a matter of a certain sense of peace, or moral strength that, even if intensive, cannot be so sharply distinguished from the effects produced by the actual psychical or moral dispositions of the subject. This is why visions that are woven into the life of a soul raised to mystical contemplation are safer than the others.

Hence, there are cases in which examination of the spiritual effects can indicate sufficiently clearly the source of the visions. Once the hand of God is recognized in the results produced, it can be recognized also in the instrument which He has used to produce them. When these effects amount to being a development, a passive intensification of the spiritual life, it seems that the director may be tranquil and may also assure the soul that the spirit of God is working in it.

But we must now determine precisely what such a conclusion implies. Evidently it implies the *supernatural* character of the visions: that is, they are an effect of divine grace. But we may ask ourselves whether, ipso facto, their *preternatural* character is demonstrated also. In other words, we may ask whether these good spiritual effects

[164] *Ascent*, bk. 2, chap. 31.
[165] *Castle*, Sixth Mansion, chap. 3.

produced in the soul permit us to deduce immediately that God is intervening in these visions in an altogether special manner, with the communication of an infused charismatic light and hence in a manner that is preternatural and miraculous. I do not think that these criteria, as such, give us any grounds for so thinking.

In this connection, I should like to draw attention to the fact that we make use of these same criteria not only to decide as to the origin of visions, but also to determine by what spirit a person is animated in his spiritual life. That is to say, the art of *discernment of spirits* takes its stand upon these same criteria of the divine action solely to declare that a soul is guided by a good spirit. We read in the works of the exponents of this delicate art—which is not to be confused with the infused gift called by the identical name—that in the intellect these signs are: truth, serious-mindedness, humility, docility, and discretion; in the will,[166] peace, humility, confidence, flexibility, patience, and especially purity of intention. A spiritual life marked by these characteristics and tending purely toward God appears to be guided by a good spirit; that is to say, it does not proceed from merely natural impulses, much less from the influence of the devil. It is the work of supernatural grace urging the soul on to God. This conclusion of an intervention of supernatural grace, deduced from the existence of such signs in the soul, seems well founded; but who would venture to argue from it that God is intervening with preternatural and miraculous elements? Certainly, this is not entirely excluded, but in the case, it must be verified by some other means. For one who has no other foundations to build upon than the virtuous and spiritual character of a soul's interior life, divine preternatural intervention simply remains an open question.

[166] D.T.C, art, *Discernement des esprits*, bk. 4, col. 1405.

Evidently, we may say the same thing when we apply the test of the spiritual effects in the special field of visions. We have noticed how, in St. John of the Cross, these effects take on a more sharply defined aspect that enables us to recognize them more clearly, but, in fine, they remain in the same category. When they are obviously good, they allow us to discern the divine action of sanctifying grace in that individual; that is, they allow us to deduce that these visions enter into the plan whereby God is bringing about the sanctification of the soul; but, as such, they do not prove the intervention of a preternatural element, a charismatic light, and so forth. This is a question that remains open and must be decided by other means.

I shall explain myself better by an example.

I have in my keeping the manuscript of a young woman who for years heard an interior voice suggesting to her beautiful spiritual thoughts. Her director, considering that it was all of God, wished her to write these down. The notebooks were examined by some priests, and no one detected any theological errors. As far as can be seen, the person concerned is also very virtuous, mortified, penitent, and animated by very high ideals of reparation. She seems even to lead a life that is really mystical. A great many of the thoughts communicated to her urge her to greater holiness. Many others constitute a sort of commentary on the Gospel teaching; a commentary that, at least in some places, is really beautiful. This young woman has also heard from her "voice" that these manuscripts of hers should be published.

I have read them. I cannot say I have found real doctrinal error in them. The want of coherence in the thought, however, and the wearisome repetitions clearly show a profoundly human imprint. They are very beautiful, or rather very "pious," but they rather leap from the sublime to the ridiculous. It is all very "good," and there emanates from it an earnest and continual invitation to union with God in sacrifice and love. I believe the good soul may have derived real profit from it for her personal spiritual life. But are these communications really received from on high, in a preternatural and wonderful way, in order to be published for the benefit of the faithful?

I doubt it very much, and I rather think that the writer's personal activity plays a great part in all these communications. Even granting the influence of the divine Spirit in these concepts of high spirituality, the single fact that they are dictated to the soul "as by a third person" does not convince me that a charismatic enlightening has intervened that would make such manifestations thereof specifically divine. In fact, when treating of the interior words that he calls "successive," St. John of the Cross has expressly remarked that when the understanding of a soul is recollected and absorbed in some consideration, it is often "helped by the Holy Spirit to produce and form these true reasonings, words and conceptions. And thus it utters them to itself as though to a third person." "And yet," adds the saint, "for the most part it is the human spirit that is working."[167] It seems to me that the meditations of the writer I have mentioned, upon the words of the Gospel, could be of this kind. Hence, there would be an influence of the Holy Spirit—for example, an enlightening of the gift of understanding—but the thoughts would remain really those of the writer. There would be no question of an objective and charismatic revelation.

You will say perhaps, "But she hears an interior voice! That, at least, is a preternatural phenomenon. Seeing that subsequently the spirit of the subject is good, this phenomenon must be attributed to God. Consequently, we have a specifically divine intervention."

Not even this can be maintained with certainty. In the present state of the psychological sciences, in view of data that may be reasonably expected, it must be maintained that the mechanism

[167] *Ascent*, bk. 2, chap. 29.

of the interior voice may sometimes be natural.[168] Unless we succeed in disproving this hypothesis, we cannot conclude that God has certainly intervened.

Consequently, I should think that this young woman's directors, even though not mistaken as to the goodness of her spirit, have attached too much importance to the revelations, maintaining that concepts and reasonings that are, for the most part, human are divine. They may be very useful for her, but I do not think they have the same utility for the public, and therefore when it is a question of carrying out the order that the writer believes she has received from God to publish these manuscripts of hers, I should prefer to judge of them according to St. John's method. I should examine the advisability of their publication "in the light of reason and faith," and since these writings seem to me decidedly inferior and tedious in form, I should have no scruple in not obeying the "divine command" intimated to the writer by her interior voice and should advise her instead to give up a tiring task that I consider useless. Does not that seem reasonable?

So far, it remains plain that it is not enough to have recognized by the spiritual results produced by the revelations that the subject is led by a good spirit, in order to be able to decide that all his revelations are specifically divine. Before we conclude in such cases that—to use the expression of a recent writer—"it is a question not of a mystic vision but of an express revelation, which we may be certain is divinely revealed," and in which "even the words are revealed," we must have something more!

Once more, we have emphasized how difficult it is to decide as to the quality of visions; yet our little excursion into the realms

[168] R. Dalbiez, "Le problème philosophique de l'hallucination," *Etudes carmélitaines* (October 1934): 133-140.

of the criteria of their authenticity will not have been useless. The director will have found there how to make sure as to the quality of the "spirit" that animates and inspires his spiritual child, so as to be able to tranquilize the latter by recognizing the hand of God even in the visions. The difficulty continues to lie only in going further—that is, in pronouncing as to the preternatural character of a vision and deciding as to its structure. But this difficulty will have shown more clearly than ever how right is St. John in never permitting a soul to ground its spiritual life upon visions and finally to summon every action enjoined by such means to the bar of reason.

Conclusion

Having come to the end of our study, we may decide precisely how far the director should be able to answer the question of the qualification of visions in order to fulfill his office perfectly. We now know that the attitude he should take up with regard to these phenomena does not depend at all on deciding as to their origin and structure. St. John of the Cross has been able to point out the most reasonable attitude for him, and the most profitable for souls, by taking his stand on the principles of spiritual theology and on the general character of visions only—that is, upon the great danger of illusions in their connection and upon their function in the spiritual life. In order to guide souls in the best way, the director need not be a specialist, able to investigate the inner structure of all these graces; it suffices that he should realize that they are of secondary importance and that the spiritual life must not depend on them but must be grounded entirely upon faith and sound theology.

Accordingly, he will help the souls entrusted to him to disregard these phenomena in order to attend more completely to the object of their faith. He will teach them to intensify their recollection in God as soon as such phenomena are observed and to profit by the grace that accompanies every true vision, urging the soul to draw nearer to Him. All this he can do without forming any opinion as to the origin of his penitent's experience. Furthermore, even without such an opinion, he can lay down the fitting attitude to take up should a command be received by means of a revelation; for all these orders must be summoned to the bar of reason enlightened by faith.

Nevertheless, it is advisable that he should know, at least with reasonable probability, that his penitent is not being misled by the devil or by his own fantastic imagination but is really led by the Spirit of God. Seeing there is question of so limited an opinion as to the quality of the visions, the spiritual effects that they produce in the soul will often furnish him with sufficiently strong grounds for remaining tranquil himself and reassuring his penitent.

If, on the other hand, we wish to decide as to the preternatural character of a vision, we enter upon a field of very delicate investigation, in which no one can reach certainty without very accurate study. But such need be undertaken only in very rare cases. We must not believe easily that God is leading a certain soul by a way that is preternatural, extraordinary, or miraculous; and it is not wise to be too ready to spend time in examining into the probability of such a state of things. It behooves the director to reserve the best of his energies and his time to guide souls along the safe path of virtue, not to investigate the possibility of extraordinary happenings. This also is a conclusion drawn from the teaching of St. John of the Cross. The latter has admirably shown how the way—the highest way—that leads to sanctity, to union with God, and to that pure love that is more profitable to Holy Church than all external works,[169] is the way of faith, which consists in the ever-more-perfect practice of the theological virtues. Too many souls still dream about "extraordinary ways" and "special missions." Often this is because they have never grasped the depths of beauty of the life of supernatural grace, never realized the grandeur of the mission that belongs to every contemplative soul. Their self-centeredness is the result of their ignorance, unless it arises—which is still worse—from a hidden spiritual conceit that is not content to walk the beaten path trodden by others.

It is enough to shrug our shoulders at such folly, but the Mystical Doctor brings us light for the benefit of all.

By demonstrating that extraordinary graces and charismata are merely accidents in the supernatural life, whereas its substantial development is founded upon the theological virtues, he has corrected the false conceptions that exaggerate the value of particular favors and lessen esteem for our true spiritual riches. The mystical union with Christ that is derived from grace is of immensely greater value than a vision in which Our Lord offers a soul the marriage ring. The vision is a symbol, a figure expressing the union; but it is grace that brings that union about. The vocation of the contemplative life gives a soul a mission more profound, and safer, than all the invitations that it may receive from supernatural locutions. If these have any value, it will be insofar as they arouse the soul to a sense of its personal vocation, which, more than all locutions, calls it to a life of loving sacrifice in union with our Redeemer. By clearly separating the field of visions from that of the substantial development of the spiritual life, by combating in souls all desire for the former, and nourishing their attraction instead for the theological virtues, St. John of the Cross has rendered them an

---

[169] *Spiritual Canticle*, stanza 29.

immense service. He has taught them not to prefer the shadow to the substance. The profound theologian of the spiritual life has mapped out for souls the safe road that, without deviations and meanderings, leads more quickly to the goal of union with God.

Convinced of the soundness of his doctrine, we shall willingly renounce all visions in order to plunge ourselves into the depths of faith, hope, and charity. Yet one day, even the theological virtues are going to end in a vision; but it will no longer be the frail visions of Earth, which we prefer to avoid, but the crowning of our whole spiritual life for all eternity: the Beatific Vision.

Appendix I

Recent Magisterial Teaching on the Discernment of Visions and Revelations

1. William Cardinal Levada, prefect of the Congregation for the Doctrine of the Faith, preface to the *Norms regarding the Manner of Proceeding in the Discernment of Presumed Apparitions or Revelations*

1. The Congregation for the Doctrine of the Faith is competent in questions regarding the promotion and safeguarding of the teaching of faith and morals. It is also competent to examine difficulties regarding the proper understanding of the faith, such as cases of pseudo-mysticism, presumed apparitions, visions and messages attributed to supernatural sources. In regard to these very delicate tasks, more than thirty years ago this Dicastery prepared the *Normae de modo procedendi in diudicandis praesumptis apparitionibus ac revelationibus*. This document, formulated by the Members of the Plenary Session of the Congregation, was approved by the Servant of God, Pope Paul VI, on 24 February 1978, and subsequently issued on 25 February 1978. At that time the *Norms* were sent to Bishops for their information, without, however, being officially published, as the norms were given for the direct aid of the Pastors of the Church.

2. Over the years this document has been published in various works treating these matters, in more than one language, without obtaining the prior permission of this Dicastery. Today, it must be recognized that the contents of these important norms are already in the public domain. Therefore, the Congregation for the Doctrine of the Faith believes it is now opportune to publish these *Norms*, providing translations in the principal languages.

3. In the Ordinary Assembly of the Synod of Bishops on the Word of God held in October 2008, the issue of the problems stemming from the experience of supernatural phenomena was raised as a pastoral concern by some Bishops. Their concern was recognized by the Holy Father, Benedict XVI, who inserted the issue into the larger context of the economy of salvation, in a significant passage of the Post-Synodal Apostolic Exhortation, *Verbum Domini*. It is important to recall this teaching of the Pontiff, which is an invitation to pay appropriate attention to these supernatural phenomena:

> In all of this, the Church gives voice to her awareness that with Jesus Christ she stands before the definitive word of God: he is *"the first and the last"* (Rev 1:17). He has given creation and history their definitive meaning; and hence we are called to live in time and in God's creation within this eschatological rhythm of the word; "thus the Christian dispensation, since it is the new and definitive covenant, will never pass away; and no new public revelation is to be expected before the glorious manifestation of our Lord Jesus Christ (cf. 1 Tim 6:14 and Tit 2:13)". Indeed, as the Fathers noted during the Synod, the "uniqueness of Christianity is manifested in the event which is Jesus Christ, the culmination of revelation, the fulfilment of God's promises

and the mediator of the encounter between man and God. He who '*has made God known*' (Jn 1:18) is the one, definitive word given to mankind." Saint John of the Cross expresses this truth magnificently: "Since he has given us his Son, his only word (for he possesses no other), he spoke everything at once in this sole word—and he has no more to say … because what he spoke before to the prophets in parts, he has spoken all at once by giving us this All who is his Son. Any person questioning God or desiring some vision or revelation would be guilty not only of foolish behaviour but also of offending him, by not fixing his eyes entirely on Christ and by living with the desire for some other novelty" (*Ascent of Mount Carmel*, II, 22).

Bearing this in mind, the Holy Father, Benedict XVI, notes the following:

Consequently the Synod pointed to the need to "help the faithful to distinguish the word of God from private revelations" whose role "is not to complete Christ's definitive revelation, but to help live more fully by it in a certain period of history." The value of private revelations is essentially different from that of the one public revelation: the latter demands faith; in it God himself speaks to us through human words and the mediation of the living community of the Church. The criterion for judging the truth of a private revelation is its orientation to Christ himself. If it leads us away from him, then it certainly does not come from the Holy Spirit, who guides us more deeply into the Gospel, and not away from it. Private revelation is an aid to this faith, and it demonstrates its credibility precisely because it refers back to the one public revelation. Ecclesiastical approval of a private revelation essentially means that its message contains nothing contrary to faith and morals; it is licit to make it public and the faithful are authorized to give to it their prudent adhesion. A private revelation can introduce new emphases, give rise to new forms of piety, or deepen older ones. It can have a certain prophetic character (cf. 1 Th 5:19-21) and can be a valuable aid for better understanding and living the Gospel at a certain time; consequently it should not be treated lightly. It is a help which is proffered, but its use is not obligatory. In any event, it must be a matter of nourishing faith, hope and love, which are for everyone the permanent path of salvation."[170]

4. It is my firm hope that the official publication of the *Norms regarding the manner of proceeding in the discernment of presumed apparitions or revelations* can aid the Pastors of the Catholic Church in their difficult task of discerning presumed apparitions, revelations, messages or, more generally, extraordinary phenomena of presumed supernatural origin. At the same time it is hoped that this text might be useful to theologians and experts in this field of the lived experience of the Church, whose delicacy requires an ever-more-thorough consideration.

William Cardinal Levada
Prefect
Vatican City State, 14 December 2011,
Feast of St. John of the Cross

---

[170] *Verbum Domini*, no. 14: AAS 102 (2010) 695-696. See also those passages of the *Catechism of the Catholic Church* dedicated to this topic (nn. 66-67).

2. Congregation for the Doctrine of the Faith, Norms regarding the Manner of Proceeding in the Discernment of Presumed Apparitions or Revelations

Preliminary Note

Origin and character of these norms

During the annual Plenary Session in November 1974, the Fathers of this Sacred Congregation examined the problems relative to presumed apparitions and to the revelations often connected with them and reached the following conclusions:

1. Today, more than in the past, news of these apparitions is diffused rapidly among the faithful thanks to the means of information (*mass media*). Moreover, the ease of going from one place to another fosters frequent pilgrimages, so that Ecclesiastical Authority should discern quickly about the merits of such matters.

2. On the other hand, modern mentality and the requirements of critical scientific investigation render it more difficult, if not almost impossible, to achieve with the required speed the judgments that in the past concluded the investigation of such matters (*constat de supernaturalitate, non constat de supernaturalitate*) and that offered to the Ordinaries the possibility of authorizing or prohibiting public cult or other forms of devotion among the faithful.

For these reasons, in order that the devotion stirred among the faithful as a result of facts of this sort might manifest itself in full communion with the Church, and bear fruits by which the Church herself might later discern the true nature of the facts, the Fathers judged that in this matter the following procedure should be promoted.

Visions and Revelations

When Ecclesiastical Authority is informed of a presumed apparition or revelation, it will be its responsibility:

a) First, to judge the fact according to positive and negative criteria (cf. *infra*, no. I);

b) Then, if this examination results in a favorable conclusion, to permit some public manifestation of cult or of devotion, overseeing this with great prudence (equivalent to the formula, "for now, nothing stands in the way") (*pro nunc nihil obstare*);

c) Finally, in light of time passed and of experience, with special regard to the fecundity of spiritual fruit generated from this new devotion, to express a judgment regarding the authenticity and supernatural character if the case so merits.

I. Criteria for Judging, at Least with Probability, the Character of the Presumed Apparitions or Revelations

A) *Positive Criteria:*

a) Moral certitude, or at least great probability of the existence of the fact, acquired by means of a serious investigation;

b) Particular circumstances relative to the existence and to the nature of the fact, that is to say:

1. Personal qualities of the subject or of the subjects (in particular, psychological equilibrium, honesty and rectitude of moral life, sincerity and habitual docility towards Ecclesiastical Authority, the capacity to return to a normal regimen of a life of faith, etc.);

2. As regards revelation: true theological and spiritual doctrine and immune from error;

3. Healthy devotion and abundant and constant spiritual fruit (for example, spirit of prayer, conversion, testimonies of charity, etc.).

B) *Negative Criteria:*

a) Manifest error concerning the fact.

b) Doctrinal errors attributed to God himself, or to the Blessed Virgin Mary, or to some saint in their manifestations, taking into account however the possibility that the subject might have added, even unconsciously, purely human elements or some error of the natural order to an authentic supernatural revelation (cf. Saint Ignatius, *Exercises*, no. 336).

c) Evidence of a search for profit or gain strictly connected to the fact.

d) Gravely immoral acts committed by the subject or his or her followers when the fact occurred or in connection with it.

e) Psychological disorder or psychopathic tendencies in the subject, that with certainty influenced on the presumed supernatural fact, or psychosis, collective hysteria or other things of this kind.

It is to be noted that these criteria, be they positive or negative, are not peremptory but rather indicative, and they should be applied cumulatively or with some mutual convergence.

II. Intervention of the Competent Ecclesiastical Authority
1. If, on the occasion of a presumed supernatural fact, there arises in a spontaneous way among the faithful a certain cult or some devotion, the competent Ecclesiastical Authority has the serious duty of looking into it without delay and of diligently watching over it.

2. If the faithful request it legitimately (that is, in communion with the Pastors, and not prompted by a sectarian spirit), the competent Ecclesiastical Authority can intervene to permit or promote some form of cult or devotion, if, after the application of the above criteria, nothing stands in the way. They must be careful that the faithful not interpret this practice as approval of the supernatural nature of the fact on the part of the Church (cf. Preliminary note c).

3. By reason of its doctrinal and pastoral task, the competent Authority can intervene *motu proprio* and indeed must do so in grave circumstances, for example, in order to correct or prevent abuses in the exercise of cult and devotion, to condemn erroneous doctrine, to avoid the dangers of a false or unseemly mysticism, etc.

4. In doubtful cases that clearly do not put the good of the Church at risk, the competent Ecclesiastical Authority is to refrain from any judgment and from any direct action (because it can also happen that, after a certain period of time, the presumed supernatural fact falls into oblivion); it must not however cease from being vigilant by intervening if necessary, with promptness and prudence.

III. *Authorities Competent to Intervene*

1. Above all, the duty of vigilance and intervention falls to the Ordinary of the place.

2. The regional or national Conference of Bishops can intervene:

    a) If the Ordinary of the place, having done his part, turns to it to judge the matter with greater certainty;

    b) If the matter pertains to the national or regional level; always, however, with the prior consent of the Ordinary of the place.

3. The Apostolic See can intervene if asked either by the Ordinary himself, by a qualified group of the faithful, or even directly by reason of the universal jurisdiction of the Supreme Pontiff (cf. *infra*, no. IV).

IV. On the Intervention of the Sacred Congregation for the Doctrine of the Faith

1. a) The intervention of the Sacred Congregation can be requested either by the Ordinary, after he has done his part, or by a qualified group of the faithful. In this second case, care must be taken that recourse to the Sacred Congregation not be motivated by suspect reasons (for example, in order to compel the Ordinary to modify his own legitimate decisions, to support some sectarian group, etc.).

b) It is up to the Sacred Congregation to intervene *motu proprio* in graver cases, especially if the matter affects the larger part of the Church, always after having consulted the Ordinary and even, if the situation requires, the Conference of Bishops.

2. It is up to the Sacred Congregation to judge and approve the Ordinary's way of proceeding or, in so far as it be possible and fitting, to initiate a new examination of the matter, distinct from that undertaken by the Ordinary and carried out either by the Sacred Congregation itself or by a special Commission.

The Present Norms, deliberated in the Plenary Session of this Sacred Congregation, were approved by the Supreme Pontiff Paul VI on 24 February 1978.

In Rome, from the palace of the Sacred Congregation for the Doctrine of the Faith, 25 February 1978.

Francis Cardinal Šeper
Prefect
Jérôme Hamer, O.P.
Secretary

3. Excerpt of Joseph Cardinal Ratzinger's Theological Commentary on the Third Secret of Fatima

A careful reading of the text of the so-called third "secret" of Fatima, published here in its entirety long after the fact and by decision of the Holy Father, will probably prove disappointing or surprising after all the speculation it has stirred. No great mystery is revealed; nor is the future unveiled. We see the Church of the martyrs of the century which has just passed represented in a scene described in a language which is symbolic and not easy to decipher. Is this what the Mother of the Lord wished to communicate to Christianity and to humanity at a time of great difficulty and distress? Is it of any help to us at the beginning of the new millennium? Or are these only projections of the inner world of children, brought up in a climate of profound piety but shaken at the same time by the tempests which threatened their own time? How should we understand the vision? What are we to make of it?

Public Revelation and private revelations – their theological status

Before attempting an interpretation, the main lines of which can be found in the statement read by Cardinal Sodano on 13 May of this year at the end of the Mass celebrated by the Holy Father in Fatima, there is a need for some basic clarification of the way in which, according to Church teaching, phenomena such as Fatima are to be understood within the life of faith. The teaching of the Church distinguishes between "public Revelation" and "private revelations". The two realities differ not only in degree but also in essence. The term "public Revelation" refers to the revealing action of God directed to humanity as a whole and which finds its literary expression in the two parts of the Bible: the Old and New Testaments. It is called "Revelation" because in it God gradually made himself known to men, to the point of becoming man himself, in order to draw to himself the whole world and unite it with himself through his Incarnate Son, Jesus Christ. It is not a matter therefore of intellectual communication, but of a life-giving process in which God comes to meet man. At the same time this process naturally produces data pertaining to the mind and to the understanding of the mystery of God. It is a process which involves man in his entirety and therefore reason as well, but not reason alone. Because God is one, history, which he shares with humanity, is also one. It is valid for all time, and it has reached its fulfilment in the life, death and resurrection of Jesus Christ. In Christ, God has said everything, that is, he has revealed himself completely, and therefore Revelation came to an end with the fulfilment of the mystery of Christ as enunciated in the New Testament. To explain the finality and completeness of Revelation, the *Catechism of the Catholic Church* quotes a text of Saint John of the Cross:

> In giving us his Son, his only Word (for he possesses no other), he spoke everything to us at once in this sole Word—and he has no more to say ... because what he spoke before to the prophets in parts, he has now spoken all at once by giving us the All Who is His Son. Any person questioning God or desiring some vision or revelation would be guilty not only of foolish behaviour but also of offending him, by not fixing his eyes entirely upon Christ and by living with the desire for some other novelty" (no. 65; St. John of the Cross, *The Ascent of Mount Carmel*, II, 22).

Because the single Revelation of God addressed to all peoples comes to completion with Christ and the witness borne to him in the books of the New Testament, the Church is tied to this unique event of sacred history and to the word of the Bible, which guarantees and interprets it. But this does not mean that the Church can now look only to the past and that she is condemned to sterile repetition. The *Catechism of the Catholic Church* says in this regard: "... even if Revelation is already complete, it has not been made fully explicit; it remains for Christian faith gradually to grasp its full significance over the course of the centuries" (no. 66). The way in which the Church is bound to both the uniqueness of the event and progress in understanding it is very well illustrated in the farewell discourse of the Lord when, taking leave of his disciples, he says:

> I have yet many things to say to you, but you cannot bear them now. When the Spirit of truth comes, he will guide you into all the truth; for he will not speak on his own authority.... He will glorify me, for he will take what is mine and declare it to you" (Jn 16:12-14).

On the one hand, the Spirit acts as a guide who discloses a knowledge previously unreachable because the premise was missing—this is the boundless breadth and depth of Christian faith. On the other hand, to be guided by the Spirit is also "to draw from" the riches of Jesus Christ himself, the inexhaustible depths of which appear in the way the Spirit leads. In this regard, the *Catechism* cites profound words of Pope Gregory the Great: "The sacred Scriptures grow with the one who reads them" (no. 94; Gregory the Great, *Homilia in Ezechielem*, I, 7, 8). The Second Vatican Council notes three essential ways in which the Spirit guides in the Church, and therefore three ways in which "the word grows": through the meditation and study of the faithful, through the deep understanding which comes from spiritual experience, and through the preaching of "those who, in the succession of the episcopate, have received the sure charism of truth" (*Dei Verbum*, 8).

In this context, it now becomes possible to understand rightly the concept of "private revelation", which refers to all the visions

and revelations which have taken place since the completion of
the New Testament. This is the category to which we must assign
the message of Fatima. In this respect, let us listen once again to
the *Catechism of the Catholic Church*: "Throughout the ages, there
have been so-called 'private' revelations, some of which have been
recognized by the authority of the Church.... It is not their role
to complete Christ's definitive Revelation, but to help live more
fully by it in a certain period of history" (no. 67). This clarifies
two things:

1. The authority of private revelations is essentially different
    from that of the definitive public Revelation. The latter
    demands faith; in it in fact God himself speaks to us
    through human words and the mediation of the living
    community of the Church. Faith in God and in his word
    is different from any other human faith, trust or opinion.
    The certainty that it is God who is speaking gives me the
    assurance that I am in touch with truth itself. It gives me
    a certitude which is beyond verification by any human
    way of knowing. It is the certitude upon which I build
    my life and to which I entrust myself in dying.

2. Private revelation is a help to this faith, and shows its
    credibility precisely by leading me back to the definitive
    public Revelation. In this regard, Cardinal Prospero Lam-
    bertini, the future Pope Benedict XIV, says in his classic
    treatise, which later became normative for beatifications
    and canonizations: "An assent of Catholic faith is not
    due to revelations approved in this way; it is not even
    possible. These revelations seek rather an assent of hu-
    man faith in keeping with the requirements of prudence,
    which puts them before us as probable and credible to
    piety". The Flemish theologian E. Dhanis, an eminent

scholar in this field, states succinctly that ecclesiastical approval of a private revelation has three elements: the message contains nothing contrary to faith or morals; it is lawful to make it public; and the faithful are authorized to accept it with prudence.[171] Such a message can be a genuine help in understanding the Gospel and living it better at a particular moment in time; therefore it should not be disregarded. It is a help which is offered, but which one is not obliged to use.

The criterion for the truth and value of a private revelation is therefore its orientation to Christ himself. When it leads us away from him, when it becomes independent of him or even presents itself as another and better plan of salvation, more important than the Gospel, then it certainly does not come from the Holy Spirit, who guides us more deeply into the Gospel and not away from it. This does not mean that a private revelation will not offer new emphases or give rise to new devotional forms, or deepen and spread older forms. But in all of this there must be a nurturing of faith, hope and love, which are the unchanging path to salvation for everyone. We might add that private revelations often spring from popular piety and leave their stamp on it, giving it a new impulse and opening the way for new forms of it. Nor does this exclude that they will have an effect even on the liturgy, as we see for instance in the feasts of Corpus Christi and of the Sacred Heart of Jesus. From one point of view, the relationship between Revelation and private revelations appears in the relationship between the liturgy and popular piety: the liturgy is the criterion, it is the living form of the Church as a whole, fed directly by the Gospel. Popular piety is

[171] E. Dhanis, "Sguardo su Fatima e bilancio di una discussione," in *La Civiltà Cattolica* 104 (1953), II, 392–406, in particular, 397.

a sign that the faith is spreading its roots into the heart of a people in such a way that it reaches into daily life. Popular religiosity is the first and fundamental mode of "inculturation" of the faith. While it must always take its lead and direction from the liturgy, it in turn enriches the faith by involving the heart.

We have thus moved from the somewhat negative clarifications, initially needed, to a positive definition of private revelations. How can they be classified correctly in relation to Scripture? To which theological category do they belong? The oldest letter of Saint Paul which has been preserved, perhaps the oldest of the New Testament texts, the First Letter to the Thessalonians, seems to me to point the way. The Apostle says: "*Do not quench the Spirit, do not despise prophesying, but test everything, holding fast to what is good*" (5:19-21). In every age the Church has received the charism of prophecy, which must be scrutinized but not scorned. On this point, it should be kept in mind that prophecy in the biblical sense does not mean to predict the future but to explain the will of God for the present, and therefore show the right path to take for the future. A person who foretells what is going to happen responds to the curiosity of the mind, which wants to draw back the veil on the future. The prophet speaks to the blindness of will and of reason, and declares the will of God as an indication and demand for the present time. In this case, prediction of the future is of secondary importance. What is essential is the actualization of the definitive Revelation, which concerns me at the deepest level. The prophetic word is a warning or a consolation, or both together. In this sense there is a link between the charism of prophecy and the category of "the signs of the times", which Vatican II brought to light anew: "*You know how to interpret the appearance of earth and sky; why then do you not know how to interpret the present time?*" (Lk 12:56). In this saying of Jesus, the "signs of the times" must be understood as the path he was taking, indeed it must be understood as Jesus himself. To interpret the signs of the times in the light of faith means to recognize the presence of Christ in every age. In the private revelations approved by the Church—and therefore also in Fatima—this is the point: they help us to understand the signs of the times and to respond to them rightly in faith.

The anthropological structure of private revelations

In these reflections we have sought so far to identify the theological status of private revelations. Before undertaking an interpretation of the message of Fatima, we must still attempt briefly to offer some clarification of their anthropological (psychological) character. In this field, theological anthropology distinguishes three forms of perception or "vision": vision with the senses, and hence exterior bodily perception, interior perception, and spiritual vision (*visio sensibilis — imaginativa — intellectualis*). It is clear that in the visions of Lourdes, Fatima and other places it is not a question of normal exterior perception of the senses: the images and forms which are seen are not located spatially, as is the case, for example, with a tree or a house. This is perfectly obvious, for instance, as regards the vision of hell (described in the first part of the Fatima "secret") or even the vision described in the third part of the "secret". But the same can be very easily shown with regard to other visions, especially since not everybody present saw them, but only the "visionaries". It is also clear that it is not a matter of a "vision" in the mind, without images, as occurs at the higher levels of mysticism. Therefore we are dealing with the middle category, interior perception. For the visionary, this perception certainly has the force of a presence, equivalent for that person to an external manifestation to the senses.

Interior vision does not mean fantasy, which would be no more than an expression of the subjective imagination. It means rather that the soul is touched by something real, even if beyond the senses. It is rendered capable of seeing that which is beyond the senses, that which cannot be seen—seeing by means of the "interior senses". It involves true "objects", which touch the soul, even if these "objects" do not belong to our habitual sensory world. This is why there is a need for an interior vigilance of the heart, which is usually precluded by the intense pressure of external reality and of the images and thoughts which fill the soul. The person is led beyond pure exteriority and is touched by deeper dimensions of reality, which become visible to him. Perhaps this explains why children tend to be the ones to receive these apparitions: their souls are as yet little disturbed, their interior powers of perception are still not impaired. "*On the lips of children and of babes you have found praise,*" replies Jesus with a phrase of Psalm 8 (v. 3) to the criticism of the High Priests and elders, who had judged the children's cries of "hosanna" inappropriate (cf. Mt 21:16).

"Interior vision" is not fantasy but, as we have said, a true and valid means of verification. But it also has its limitations. Even in exterior vision the subjective element is always present. We do not see the pure object, but it comes to us through the filter of our senses, which carry out a work of translation. This is still more evident in the case of interior vision, especially when it involves realities which in themselves transcend our horizon. The subject, the visionary, is still more powerfully involved. He sees insofar as he is able, in the modes of representation and consciousness available to him. In the case of interior vision, the process of translation is even more extensive than in exterior vision, for the subject shares in an essential way in the formation of the image of what appears. He can arrive at the image only within the bounds of his capacities and possibilities. Such visions therefore are never simple "photographs" of the other world, but are influenced by the potentialities and limitations of the perceiving subject.

This can be demonstrated in all the great visions of the saints; and naturally it is also true of the visions of the children at Fatima. The images described by them are by no means a simple expression of their fantasy, but the result of a real perception of a higher and interior origin. But neither should they be thought of as if for a moment the veil of the other world were drawn back, with heaven appearing in its pure essence, as one day we hope to see it in our definitive union with God. Rather the images are, in a manner of speaking, a synthesis of the impulse coming from on high and the capacity to receive this impulse in the visionaries, that is, the children. For this reason, the figurative language of the visions is symbolic. In this regard, Cardinal Sodano stated: "[They] do not describe photographically the details of future events, but synthesize and compress against a single background facts which extend through time in an unspecified succession and duration". This compression of time and place in a single image is typical of such visions, which for the most part can be deciphered only in retrospect. Not every element of the vision has to have a specific historical sense. It is the vision as a whole that matters, and the details must be understood on the basis of the images taken in their entirety. The central element of the image is revealed where it coincides with what is the focal point of Christian "prophecy" itself: the center is found where the vision becomes a summons and a guide to the will of God.[172]

---

[172] The entire text of the Third Secret of Fatima and its commentaries can be found on the Vatican website: https://www.vatican.va/roman_curia/congregations/cfaith/documents/rc_con_cfaith_doc_20000626_message-fatima_en.html or https://www.ewtn.com/catholicism/library/message-of-fatima-2045.

Appendix II

Other Pastoral Considerations in the Discernment of Visions and Revelations

Taken from Antonio Royo Marín, O.P., and Jordan Aumann, O.P., *The Theology of Christian Perfection* (Dubuque, IA: The Priory Press, 1962) 662–663, 651–653.

1. Rules of Discernment of Mystical Phenomena

The following norms are offered as rules by which the spiritual director may be guided in the discernment of spirits so far as it pertains to revelations and prophecies:

1. Any revelation contrary to faith and morals must be rejected as false. God does not contradict himself.

2. Any revelation contrary to the common teaching of theologians or purporting to settle an argument among the schools of theology should be held as gravely suspect. Most authors maintain that it must be rejected, but Pope Benedict XIV, while referring to both opinions, does not settle the question.[173]

---

[173] Pope Benedict XIV, *De Servorum Dei*, Lib III, final chapter. See also Bl. Pius IX, *Tuas Libenter* – Letter to the Archbishop of Munich-Freising (December 21, 1863), (Denz. 2875–2880)

3. Just because one aspect of the revelation is found to be false does not serve as grounds to reject the entire revelation; the remainder of what is revealed can possibly be authentic.

4. The fact that a given prophecy is fulfilled is not a conclusive argument for the divine origin of a revelation. This could have been brought about by a natural cause or as the result of a superior natural knowledge given to the seer.

5. Revelations concerning curious or useless matters or those that are overly detailed, lengthy, and filled with a plethora of proofs and reasons should be rejected as not of God. Divine Revelations are usually clear, brief, and precise.

6. Every person who receives a revelation should be examined carefully, especially as to temperament and character. If a person is humble, well balanced, discreet, evidently advanced in virtue, and enjoys good mental and physical health, there is good reason to proceed further and to examine the revelation itself. But if the individual is exhausted with excessive mortifications, suffers nervous affliction, is subject to periods of great exhaustion or great depression, or is eager to divulge the revelation, there is cause for serious doubt.

7. Lastly, the principal rule of discernment is to judge the revelation by the fruits it produces in the soul of the individual, yet always understanding the revelation is as such a charism and, therefore, primarily for the good of others

---

as well as Fr. Chad Ripperger, *The Consensus of the Fathers and Theologians* (N.p.: Sensus Traditionis Press, 2020) for a further understanding of the importance of Theological Consensus.

and, moreover, that it is always possible for an individual to use the gifts of God to his own spiritual detriment.

2. Diabolical Influence

The study of the preternatural is so vast and complicated that a thorough treatment of the subject would take us far beyond the scope of the present work. We shall content ourselves with enumeration of the main points of theological doctrine concerning diabolical influence and refer the reader to other works which treat the subject in greater detail.[174]

1. It is *de fide* that devils exist, that is, a number of angels who were created good by God but became evil through their own sin.[175]

2. With God's permission the devils can exercise an evil influence over men, even to the extent of invading and tormenting them in a bodily manner.[176]

3. In the midst of the assaults of the devil, man's will always remains free, because the will can be moved only in two ways: by the individual himself or by God. The most that any other extrinsic power can do is to persuade; this is what the devils do.[177]

4. The good angels and devils can intrinsically act upon the imagination and other internal and external senses because these are all organic powers and the devil has power to exercise his influence on anything material.[178]

[174] Cf. *Satan*, ed. Bruno de Jesus-Marie, OCD (New York: Sheed and Ward, 1952).
[175] Cf. Matt. 25:41; 2 Pet. 2:4; Fourth Lateran Council (Denz 428).
[176] Cf. Eph. 6:11-12; 1 Thess. 3:5; 1 Pet. 5:8-9.
[177] Cf. St. Thomas Aquinas, *Summa Theologica*, I, q. 111, art. 2.
[178] Cf. St. Thomas Aquinas, *Summa Theologica*, I, q. 111, arts. 3-4.

5. The devils cannot work through miracles, because by definition a miracle surpasses the power of all created nature. But since the angelic powers far surpassed human powers, the devils can perform prodigious feats which arouse man's admiration so far as they exceed the power or knowledge of human beings.[179]

Diabolical Limitations

By reason of some contradiction involved or because they surpassed the power of an angelic being, the devils cannot do the following:

1. Produce any kind of truly supernatural phenomenon, because the supernatural by definition exceeds all natural created powers.
2. Create a substance, because creation requires an infinite power and no creature of any kind can be used even as an instrument of creation.[180]
3. Raise a dead person to life, although he can produce the illusion of doing so.
4. Instantaneously cure wounds, fractures, lesions or other injuries. This is something only God can do.
5. Instantaneously transport a body from one place to another without passing through the intervening space, although the devil can do so himself as a pure spirit and can transport bodies with great rapidity.[181]
6. Make truly prophetic predictions since the devil does not, by his own powers of intelligence, know future contingencies, although he knows so many things in

---

[179] Cf. St. Thomas Aquinas, *Summa Theologica*, I, q. 114, art. 4.
[180] Cf. St. Thomas Aquinas, *Summa Theologica*, I, q. 45, art. 5.
[181] Cf. St. Thomas Aquinas, *Summa Theologica*, I, q. 53, art. 2.

their causes that it may appear to human beings that what was predicted was a true prophecy.

7. Know the secrets of a person's mind and heart, since the devil does not by his own power have access to the human intellect and will. Because of his superior intelligence, however, he can conjecture much more easily and know the temperament and character of individuals as well as numerous circumstances in their life.

8. Produce in human beings extraordinary phenomena of the purely intellectual or volitional type. Because he does not have free access to the human intellect and will.[182]

4. Diabolical Falsifications

The above are the principal things which the devils are unable to do, and they should be kept in mind when evaluating mystical phenomena that involve the miraculous, or the activity of the human intellect and will. The following mystical phenomena, however, can be falsified by the devil. With God's permission the devil can do any of the following:

1. Produce corporeal or imaginative visions (but not intellectual visions).

2. Falsify ecstasy.

3. Produce rays of light in the body and sensible heat (there have been examples of what is called "diabolical incandescence").

4. Cause sensible consolations and tenderness.

5. Instantaneously cure strange sicknesses which have been caused by diabolical influence, although according to

---

[182] Cf. St. Thomas Aquinas, *Summa Theologica*, I, q. 111, arts. 1–2.

Tertullian these were not authentic sicknesses in the first place and it is not so much a cure as it is that the devil ceases to torment the individual.[183]

6. Produce the stigmata and all other kinds of bodily extraordinary phenomena, and any phenomena dealing with physical objects—such as crowns, rings, etc.

7. Simulate miracles and the phenomena of levitation, bilocation, and copenetration of bodies.

8. Cause persons or objects to disappear from sight by placing an obstacle in the line of vision or acting directly on the sense of sight; simulate locutions by means of sound waves or immediate action on the sense of hearing.

9. Produce bodily incombustibility by interposing some medium between the fire and the body of the individual.

To summarize: all the phenomena which result from the activity of any natural power or physical law, even if the human being is unable to produce them, can be produced by diabolical power, with God's permission. Whatever the activity of diabolical powers, however, it will never surpass the natural order. As we have already explained, we speak of the preternatural in relation to a given phenomenon which surpasses human power but can be produced by the devil.

---

[183] Cf. Tertulllian, *Apologia*, chap. 22.

About the Author

Fr. Gabriel of St. Mary Magdalen, O.C.D. (1893–1953), was a Discalced Carmelite priest, confessor, and spiritual director. He was an expert in the writings of venerated Carmelite mystics, such as St. Teresa of Ávila and St. John of the Cross. For the last decade of his life, Fr. Gabriel was the spiritual director of the Discalced Carmelite nuns of the Monastery of St. Joseph in Rome. It was with their assistance that he compiled his writings and mystical insights, arranging his material to correspond with the liturgical year, while following the ascent of the soul to transforming union with God.

SPIRITUAL DIRECTION
⫷ SERIES ⫸

SOPHIA INSTITUTE PRESS

If this book has caused a stir in your heart to continue to pursue your relationship with God, we invite you to explore two extraordinary resources, SpiritualDirection.com and the Avila Institute for Spiritual Formation.

The readers of SpiritualDirection.com reside in almost every country of the world where hearts yearn for God. It is the world's most popular English site dedicated to authentic Catholic spirituality.

The Students of the Avila Institute for Spiritual Formation sit at the feet of the rich and deep well of the wisdom of the saints.

You can find more about the Avila Institute at
www.Avila-Institute.com.

Sophia Institute

Sophia Institute is a nonprofit institution that seeks to nurture the spiritual, moral, and cultural life of souls and to spread the gospel of Christ in conformity with the authentic teachings of the Roman Catholic Church.

Sophia Institute Press fulfills this mission by offering translations, reprints, and new publications that afford readers a rich source of the enduring wisdom of mankind.

Sophia Institute also operates the popular online resource CatholicExchange.com. *Catholic Exchange* provides world news from a Catholic perspective as well as daily devotionals and articles that will help readers to grow in holiness and live a life consistent with the teachings of the Church.

In 2013, Sophia Institute launched Sophia Institute for Teachers to renew and rebuild Catholic culture through service to Catholic education. With the goal of nurturing the spiritual, moral, and cultural life of souls, and an abiding respect for the role and work of teachers, we strive to provide materials and programs that are at once enlightening to the mind and ennobling to the heart; faithful and complete, as well as useful and practical.

Sophia Institute gratefully recognizes the Solidarity Association for preserving and encouraging the growth of our apostolate over the course of many years. Without their generous and timely support, this book would not be in your hands.

www.SophiaInstitute.com
www.CatholicExchange.com
www.SophiaInstituteforTeachers.org